Southern Living

Homemaker's Cookbook ®

CAKES

by Lena E. Sturges

Southern Living BOOKS

BIRMINGHAM, ALABAMA

Contents

Introduction

*H*ere at *Southern Living*, we believe that a cookbook should be easy to read, its instructions should be clearly stated, and its recipes should be kitchen-tested by trained professionals.

In creating the SOUTHERN LIVING HOMEMAKER'S COOKBOOK®—CAKES, we selected the best cake, frosting, and filling recipes from the thousands we have kitchen-tested over the years. Every cake selected and included in this volume has been baked in our test kitchens to be sure that temperature, time of baking, and pan size are correct.

This testing wasn't enough. The cakes still had to pass on appearance, texture, and flavor. Neighbors, co-workers, and families served on our tasting panels, who did more than merely taste. They frequently required an entire slice before arriving at a decision. We will have to admit that some cakes rated more "ahh, good" than others. This was the compliment we wanted to pass on to you. Cakes that did not pass these tests are not in this book.

After all testing was completed, we then edited the recipes very carefully so that they would be easy to follow, for the beginner and the expert alike.

We know you're eager to try these recipes. We hope you will read the instructions on the following pages before you start. If you follow directions carefully, the cake you save may be tonight's dessert.

Happy baking!

Lena E. Sturges

Section One

For Perfect Cakes Every Time

Steps for Making a Good Cake

1. **Read recipe** carefully before starting. Be sure you have all the ingredients listed, as well as the size pan called for in the recipe.

2. **Prepare baking pans** and set aside. Check recipe to see if pans need to be greased or lined with paper. Grease pan generously with unsalted shortening and flour generously. Shake excess flour from pan. Pan may be lined with baking paper or waxed paper. Grease side of pan when only bottom of pan is lined. Remove lining as soon as cake is turned onto rack to cool. Pans for sponge cakes should not be greased or floured.

3. **Assemble ingredients.** Have all ingredients at room temperature. You might chop the raisins, nuts, or dates while eggs and butter are reaching room temperature.

4. **Preheat oven.** Set oven to bake at temperature given in recipe. Unless otherwise stated in recipe, all cakes are to be baked in a preheated oven. When using oven-glass baking pans, always lower the temperature 25 degrees. If your oven temperature is not accurate, it will be necessary to adjust baking time. Accuracy of temperature is one of the most important steps in cake-making.

5. **Measure carefully.** You will need to use standard measuring spoons and cups. All measurements in these recipes are level.

To measure sugar—Fill cup with granulated sugar, level off with spatula or straight edge of a knife. Brown sugar should be packed into cup so firmly that it holds its shape when turned out of cup. Powdered sugar should be sifted before being measured.

To measure shortening—Pack shortening into cup to measure and level top with spatula. One stick of butter or margarine equals ½ cup and need not be measured. To measure melted shortening or oil, set measuring cup on a level surface so that the surface of the liquid will not be slanted.

6. **Mix as directed.** Don't take a shortcut here. There's a definite reason why ingredients are listed in the order of their addition. Keep sides of mixing bowl tidy. Use a rubber scraper so every particle can be expertly blended into the batter.

To cream ingredients—Have shortening soft, but not melted. Beat shortening until smooth, then add sugar gradually, beating until smooth. Properly creamed shortening and sugar make the cake fluffy.

To beat eggs—Be sure that beaters and bowl are free from all grease. Beat egg yolks until light and fluffy. Blend into thoroughly creamed shortening and sugar, then beat thoroughly. Beat egg whites just before you use them. Beat only until they will hold an upright peak when beater is pulled out of them. They should be fine-textured and glossy, not dry.

To fold in egg whites—Drop the beaten egg whites onto the batter, then

2

cut down through the batter with edge of spoon or spatula, turn it, and bring it up along side of bowl and fold some of the batter over the egg whites; then turn spoon and cut down again. Continue very gently until egg whites are completely distributed throughout the batter. Do not beat.

To add dry ingredients—Combined dry ingredients are usually added to creamed mixture alternately with liquid. Stir in some of dry ingredients, then a little liquid, beginning and ending with dry ingredients. Stir just enough after each addition to keep batter smooth and to blend the ingredients. Vigorous beating at this point will result in a coarse, tough cake.

7. **Put batter evenly in pans.** Remove air bubbles by gently shaking or tapping layer cake pans, or by cutting through batter with a knife in loaf or tube pans.

8. **Place cake pans** in center of oven, and space them on the rack for good circulation of heat. For even browning, do not let pans touch sides of oven or each other.

9. **Set timer** and don't peek until recommended time is up. This often causes the cake to fall. Some recipes say bake 30 to 35 minutes. In this case, set timer at 30 minutes and check.

10. **Test cake** for doneness. Cake is done if: it springs back when lightly touched with the finger . . . or a toothpick comes out clean when inserted in the center . . . or cake begins to pull away from the sides of the pan.

11. **Cool cake.** Let pans sit 5 to 10 minutes before turning cake out on wire rack to cool. If pan has been properly greased, cake should slip out easily. It may be necessary to slip a knife or spatula in at side to loosen if cake does not slip out of pan easily. Turn cake right-side up to cool (by transferring from one wire rack to another).

12. **Frost cake,** if desired. Follow directions given in the "Steps for Frosting the Cake" section of this book.

13. **Freeze cake,** if necessary. As a general rule, cakes are better frozen before frosting. Cooked frostings do not freeze well at all—but a butter-powdered sugar frosting can be frozen on the cake. If you are planning to freeze the cake by layers, cool thoroughly and freeze on cardboard or cake rack. Wrap layers and frosted cakes in moisture, vaporproof material. When frosting a cake from the freezer, thaw it uncovered, then add frosting.

Ingredients for Cakes

Flour—The right kind of flour is important; don't make a substitution for the kind of flour the recipe calls for. In the recipes in this book, unless cake flour is called for, you may assume you are to use all-purpose flour. If you are using the presifted or instant-type flour, follow directions on the package for combining dry ingredients. When using self-rising flour, omit baking powder and salt from recipe. Do not substitute self-rising flour in cakes where eggs are leavening agent.

Eggs—All eggs should be fresh. We have used large eggs in all recipes in this book. Remove eggs from refrigerator several hours before using so they will beat up to their greatest volume.

Liquids—Use the liquid called for in the recipe. Sour milk or buttermilk are interchangeable. If the recipe states "milk," it means sweet milk.

Shortening—Be sure that the shortening used is fresh. Generally, margarine and butter are interchangeable unless stated in the recipe. A creamy vegetable shortening may often be substituted for butter or margarine, although the flavor will be different. Use oil or melted shortening only when the recipe calls for it. The method of mixing is usually different when oil is used.

Leavening agents—In all recipes in this book, we have used double-acting baking powder. Soda is used as leavening in some recipes; follow recipe directions for adding. Eggs provide the leavening for angel food and some pound cakes.

Chocolate and cocoa—In these recipes, unless otherwise stated, chocolate means the unsweetened kind. We do not recommend using cocoa and chocolate interchangeably, since adjustments in shortening would need to be made.

Sugar—Granulated sugar is used in all recipes unless otherwise stated. Sugars are not interchangeable so do not substitute granulated sugar for brown sugar.

Equipment for Good Cakes

Measuring cups and spoons—Level and accurate measurements are very important. To measure dry ingredients, you will need a set of measuring cups (¼, ⅓, ½, and 1 cup) or a measuring cup with those measurements on the side. A liquid measuring cup has a lip for easier pouring.

Measuring spoon sets include ¼ teaspoon, ½ teaspoon, 1 teaspoon, and 1 tablespoon.

Bowl scraper—Rubber scrapers are usually more pliable, although some of plastic are quite satisfactory.

Spatulas—Large and small spatulas have many uses in cake making and frosting. A spatula or a knife may be used to level ingredients in spoons or cups.

Mixing spoons—Wooden mixing spoons are more satisfactory than those of silver or stainless.

Electric beater or mixer—Many good cakes may be beaten by hand, but a mixer is much faster and easier.

Mixing bowls—Nested sets of mixing bowls are very handy for premeasuring, beating eggs, etc.

Cake pans—It is suggested that you have at least three 8- and 9-inch layer pans for baking. The newer, more modern, ovens are larger, and it is possible to bake three layers at one time. A 12- x 9- x 2-inch pan is preferred for sheet cakes, and 11- x 8-inch pans are handy for baking many cakes.

Loaf and tube pans vary in size. Be sure to use the recommended size for the recipe you are using. A Bundt pan may be substituted for a tube pan for most cakes. We have found the Bundt pan is not quite as good as a tube pan when you are using a recipe with a large quantity of fruits and nuts.

A jellyroll pan can serve several purposes. It can be used for making a jellyroll, for cookies, and for some sheet cakes.

Check recipe for recommended pan size. Shiny aluminum or tin pans distribute heat evenly and give more even browning.

Wire racks—Every kitchen should have at least three wire racks. They can be used for many things other than cooling cakes and cookies.

Cooking Terms

A La Mode—Served with a topping of ice cream.

Bake—To cook foods in the oven at a set temperature.

Beat—To make a mixture smooth or to introduce air by using brisk, regular motion that lifts the mixture over and over.

Beat Lightly—To stir with a fork to mix. This process usually applies to mixing the whites or yolks of eggs.

Blanch—To boil in water for a short time, or to pour boiling water over food, then drain it almost immediately.

Blend—To combine two or more ingredients by mixing thoroughly.

Boil—To cook in boiling water or liquid.

Broil—To cook by direct heat.

Brush—To spread or brush with melted fat or other liquid to coat.

Caramelize—To heat dry sugar or food containing sugar until light brown and caramel flavored.

Chill—To cool in the refrigerator or other cold place.

Coat the Spoon—To cook until a mixture adheres to the stirring spoon in a thin layer.

Cream—To work one or more foods until mixture is soft and creamy or fluffy.

Cube—To cut into small squares of equal size.

Cut in Shortening—To combine shortening with flour and other dry ingredients by chopping it into the mixture with two knives or spatulas.

Dot—To scatter small pieces of butter or other fat over food before cooking.

Dredge—To coat or sprinkle lightly with flour, sugar, etc., until food is well covered.

Fold—To combine by using two motions, cutting vertically through the mixture and turning over and over by sliding the implement across the bottom of the mixing bowl with each turn.

Glaze—To brush or pour a shiny coating over foods.

Grate—To cut food into minute particles by rubbing on a grater.

Grease—To rub lightly with shortening.

Grind—To cut food into tiny particles by putting through a food grinder.

Knead—To fold, turn, and press down on dough with the hands until it becomes smooth and elastic.

Marinate—To let foods stand in an acid-oil mixture.

Mince—To cut or chop into very small pieces.

Peel—To strip off the outside covering.

Preheat—To heat oven to desired temperature before putting food in oven.

Punch Down—To strike down risen dough with the fist to allow gas to escape and fresh oxygen to reach the yeast.

Scald—To heat milk to just below the boiling point.

Shred—To cut fine with a knife or sharp instrument.

Simmer—To cook by moist heat at a low temperature.

Sliver—To slice into long, thin strips.

Soft Peaks—To beat egg whites or whipping cream until peaks are formed when beaters are lifted, but tips curl over.

Steep—Let stand in hot liquid.

Stir—To mix foods with a circular motion for the purpose of blending or obtaining uniform consistency.

Handy Substitutions

It is always best to use the ingredient called for in the recipe, but many times it is necessary to make substitutions. For best results, use this table only when you do not have the ingredient called for in the recipe.

If Recipe Calls For	*You May Use*
1 square unsweetened chocolate	3 tablespoons cocoa plus 1 tablespoon butter or margarine
2 large eggs	3 small eggs
1 cup sifted all-purpose flour	1 cup sifted cake flour plus 2 tablespoons
1 cup sifted cake flour	1 cup sifted all-purpose flour minus 2 tablespoons
1 teaspoon baking powder	¼ teaspoon baking soda plus ½ teaspoon cream of tartar
1 cup honey	¾ cup sugar plus ¼ cup liquid
1 cup fresh sweet milk	½ cup evaporated milk plus ½ cup water
1 cup fresh sweet milk	3 to 5 tablespoons nonfat dry milk solids in 1 cup water
1 cup fresh sweet milk	1 cup sour milk plus ½ teaspoon soda (decrease baking powder 2 teaspoons)
1 cup sour milk or buttermilk	1 or 2 tablespoons lemon juice or vinegar with sweet milk to fill cup (let stand 5 minutes)
1 cup brown sugar (firmly packed)	1 cup granulated sugar
Thickening	1 tablespoon quick-cooking tapioca, or 1 tablespoon cornstarch, or 2 tablespoons flour

Equivalent Weights and Measures

Food	Weight	Measure
Apples	1 pound (3 medium)	3 cups, sliced
Bananas	1 pound (3 medium)	2½ cups, sliced about 2 cups, mashed
Bread	1 pound	12 to 16 slices

Food	Weight	Measure
Butter or Margarine	1 pound	2 cups
Butter or Margarine	¼ pound stick	½ cup
Butter or Margarine	size of an egg	about ¼ cup
Candied fruit or peels	½ pound	1¼ cups, cut
Cheese, American	1 pound	4 to 5 cups, grated
Cottage	1 pound	2 cups
Cream	3-ounce package	6 tablespoons
Cocoa	1 pound	4 cups
Coconut, flaked or shredded	1 pound	5 cups
Coffee	1 pound	80 tablespoons
Cornmeal	1 pound	3 cups
Cream, heavy	½ pint	2 cups, whipped
Dates, pitted	1 pound	2 to 3 cups, chopped
Dates, pitted	7¼-ounce package	1¼ cups, chopped
Flour		
All-purpose	1 pound	4 cups, sifted
Cake	1 pound	4¾ to 5 cups, sifted
Whole wheat	1 pound	3½ cups, unsifted
Lemon juice	1 medium	2 to 3 tablespoons
Lemon rind	1 medium	2 teaspoons, grated
Milk		
Evaporated	6-ounce can	¾ cup
Evaporated	14½-ounce can	1⅔ cups
Sweetened condensed	14-ounce can	1¼ cups
Sweetened condensed	15-ounce can	1⅓ cups
Nuts, in shell		
Almonds	1 pound	1 to 1¾ cups nutmeats
Peanuts	1 pound	2 cups nutmeats
Pecans	1 pound	2¼ cups nutmeats
Walnuts	1 pound	1⅔ cups nutmeats, chopped
Nuts, shelled		
Almonds	1 pound, 2 ounces	4 cups
Peanuts	1 pound	4 cups
Pecans	1 pound	4 cups
Walnuts	1 pound	3 cups
Orange juice	1 medium	⅓ cup
Orange rind	1 medium	2 tablespoons, grated
Raisins, seedless	1 pound	3 cups
Sugar		
Brown	1 pound	2¼ cups, firmly packed
Powdered	1 pound	3½ cups, unsifted
Granulated	1 pound	2 cups

Measurements

Always use standard measuring cups (both dry and liquid measure) and measuring spoons when measuring a recipe. All measurements given below are level.

3 teaspoons . . . . 1 tablespoon
4 tablespoons . . . . ¼ cup
8 tablespoons . . . . ½ cup
16 tablespoons . . . . .1 cup
1 cup . . . . .8 fluid ounces
2 cups . . . . .1 pint (16 fluid ounces)
⅛ cup . . . . 2 tablespoons
⅓ cup . . . . .5 tablespoons plus 1 teaspoon
⅔ cup . . . . 10 tablespoons plus 2 teaspoons
¾ cup . . . . .12 tablespoons
Few grains (or dash) . . . . .less than ⅛ teaspoon
Pinch . . as much as can be taken between tip of finger and thumb

Steps for Frosting the Cake

Frosting a cake is an art. Although some homemakers are more gifted than others, almost anyone can turn out a pretty cake with a little practice. Here are some general rules to follow:

1. **Cool Cake and Frosting**
    Be sure to cool the cake and frosting before starting this step. Brush all loose crumbs from cake with a pastry brush. Keep a cover on frosting as it cools unless stated otherwise in recipe.

2. **Prepare the Cake for Frosting**
    Place the cake on a flat cake plate or tray at least 2 inches larger than the cake on all sides.
    To keep the plate or tray clean while frosting the cake, cover the outer area of plate with strips of waxed paper, extending it beyond the edge of the plate.
    Set the cake plate on rim of large mixing bowl—with plate extending beyond rim of bowl. This makes it easy to turn the cake while frosting and decorating.

3. **Frost the Single-Layer or Sheet Cake**
    Place one-layer and sheet cakes, right side up, on the cake plate. (Instructions given above in Step 2.) Frost sides and top of cake. Frostings go on top sides of cake more smoothly than on the bottom sides.

4. Frost the Two- and Three-Layer Cake

If there is a difference in the thickness of the layers, use the thickest layer on the bottom and use the smoothest layer for the top.

Turn the first layer upside down and spread with frosting or filling. Use a thin, short spatula. Then place second layer, right side up, on top of filling.

If layers have a tendency to slide, anchor them with toothpicks until the filling has set.

Continue to add layers, right side up, until all layers have been used.

5. Frosting the Top and Sides of the Cake

Frost sides of cake starting at the bottom and holding spatula in a vertical position. Completely cover sides with sweeping strokes of the spatula.

Then fill the center top and work out to the edges, making swirls with spatula, a knife, or the back of a spoon.

Let frosting set, then remove the strips of waxed paper.

Causes of Cake Failure

If This Happens	*Possible Cause In Shortening-Type Cakes*	*Possible Cause In Sponge-Type Cakes*
Cake is Undersized	Not enough leavening Used wrong type leavening Baked in too large pan Pan too hot	Under- or overbeaten egg whites or yolks Overmixing Not enough sugar Pan too large Oven too hot Cake removed from pan while hot
Cake Falls	Too much leavening Too much liquid or sugar Oven not hot enough Insufficient baking	Too much sugar Used a greased pan Oven not hot enough Too much fat Insufficient baking
Top Crust is Hard and Cracked	Oven too hot Baked too long	Same as for shortening-type cakes
Cake "Humps" in Center	Oven too hot at start of baking Too much flour Not enough liquid	Oven too hot Overbeaten egg whites Too much flour

If This Happens	Possible Cause In Shortening-Type Cakes	Possible Cause In Sponge-Type Cakes
Cake Has Soggy Streak	Undermixing Fat too soft Not enough leavening Underbeaten eggs (creaming) Too much liquid	Undermixing Too many egg yolks Underbeaten yolks
Cake Sticks to Pan or Crust Rolls Off in Balls	Cake left in pan too long Pan not greased and lined	Cake left in pan too long Oven not hot enough during last 15 minutes
Sponge-Type Cake Shrinks		Used greased pan Too much sugar Insufficient baking
Cake is Heavy	Final overmixing (where flour and liquid are added) Too much shortening Too much sugar Too much liquid Oven too hot	Under- or overbeaten eggs Overmixing Left out cream of tartar or other acid
Cake Cracks and Falls Apart	Too much shortening, leavening or sugar Removed from pan too soon	Same as for shortening-type cakes
Cake is Uneven or Unlevel	Uneven oven heat Rack or oven not level Batter not spread evenly Used a warped pan	Same as for shortening-type cakes
Cake Runs Over	Pan too full Oven too crowded Too much leavening Too much sugar	Same as for shortening-type cakes
Crust is Sticky	Too much sugar Oven not hot enough Insufficient baking	Same as for shortening-type cakes

11

If This Happens	*Possible Cause In Shortening-Type Cakes*	*Possible Cause In Sponge-Type Cakes*
Cake Has Coarse Texture	Too much leavening Inadequate mixing or creaming Shortening too soft Oven temperature too low	Under- or overbeaten eggs Ingredients not well blended Wrong kind or too much flour Oven temperature too low
Cake Has Dry Texture	Too much flour Too much leavening Not enough shortening Not enough sugar Overbeaten egg whites	Same as for shortening-type cakes

Cake Cutting Guide

Now that your cake is out of the oven and you're satisfied that it's going to be a delicious cake, a great deal will depend on the way it is cut and served.

You will need to know how many servings you will get from each cake. The guide below will give you some idea of ways in which various cakes may be cut.

A good sharp knife, with a straight thin blade, is most suitable for cutting batter cakes. Insert the point of knife into cake, keeping point down and handle up. Slice, pulling toward you in short sawing motions. Dip knife in hot water to keep from sticking.

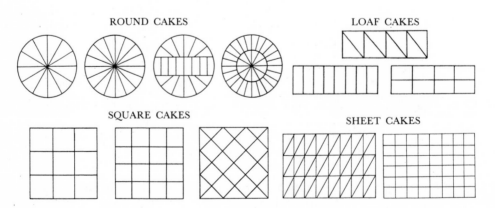

ROUND CAKES

LOAF CAKES

SQUARE CAKES

SHEET CAKES

Section Two

Cake Recipes

❧Angel Food Cake
(10- x 4½-inch tube pan)

1 cup cake flour	½ teaspoon salt
1½ cups sugar	1½ teaspoons cream of tartar
1½ cups egg whites (12 eggs)	1½ teaspoons flavoring

Sift flour and ½ cup of the sugar together four times. Set aside. Measure egg whites into large bowl; then beat to a coarse foam. Measure and sprinkle over surface of whites the salt, cream of tartar, and flavoring. Beat until whites barely hold a peak, and stop beating when whites are still moist and slightly foamy. To test, shake bowl gently; meringue should slide slightly in bowl. Add remaining 1 cup sugar in 2-tablespoon portions, sprinkling it over surface; then beating in. Fold in flour mixture in four portions gently, but thoroughly. Pile lightly in ungreased 10- x 4½-inch tube pan rinsed with cold water. Insert knife and circle batter twice to cut any air pockets. Bake at 300° about 1 hour. Touch surface lightly with fingertip; when springs from sides of pan, it is done. Invert pan and cool thoroughly, about 1 hour, before removing cake.

❧Texas Angel Cake
(tube pan)

White Part

6 egg whites	¾ cup sugar
¼ teaspoon salt	½ cup cake flour
½ teaspoon cream of tartar	½ teaspoon vanilla extract

Beat egg whites until foamy. Add salt and cream of tartar. Add sugar, 2 tablespoons at a time. Sift cake flour and add to egg whites a small amount at a time. Fold in vanilla. Pour batter into ungreased tube pan.

Yellow Part

6 egg yolks	½ teaspoon salt
¾ cup sugar	¼ cup boiling water
¾ cup cake flour	1 teaspoon lemon extract
1 teaspoon baking powder	

Beat together egg yolks and sugar until smooth and fluffy. Sift flour, baking powder, and salt together. Add flour mixture to egg mixture alternately with hot water. Add lemon extract. Place this mixture by spoonfuls on top of white mixture. Bake at 275° for 50 minutes. Increase temperature of oven to 325° and bake an additional 10 to 15 minutes. Remove from oven and invert pan on rack for 1 hour or until cold.

❦ Cocoa Angel Cake

(MEDIUM-SIZED TUBE PAN)

1 cup cake flour or ⅞ cup all-purpose flour	1 teaspoon salt
	1 cup egg whites (8 or 9 eggs)
1¼ cups sugar	¾ teaspoon cream of tartar
¼ cup cocoa	1 teaspoon flavoring

Sift flour, sugar, and cocoa thoroughly. Add salt to egg whites and beat until foamy. Add the cream of tartar and flavoring and continue beating until the whites just form a peak when the beater is drawn through. Add the dry ingredients by sifting 3 or 4 tablespoons at a time over the whites. Fold in gently with a spatula or whisk. Bake in ungreased tube pan at 300° for about 1 hour. Invert pan and cool before removing.

❦ Texas Angel Food Cake

(10-INCH TUBE PAN)

1½ cups cake flour	¼ teaspoon salt
2 teaspoons cream of tartar	1 tablespoon lemon juice
2¼ cups sugar	1 teaspoon vanilla extract
12 large egg whites	

Sift flour and measure. Add 1 teaspoon cream of tartar, and sift five times. Sift sugar and measure. Set aside. Beat egg whites until they hold up in peaks. Add salt and 1 teaspoon cream of tartar. Add sugar, 2 tablespoons at a time. Add lemon juice and vanilla. Fold in flour, 2 tablespoons at a time. Bake in a tube pan at 375° for 30 minutes and then reduce temperature to 325° and bake 30 minutes longer.

❦ Dutch Apple Cake
(9- x 9- x 2-inch pan)

⅓ cup milk
¼ cup sugar
½ teaspoon salt
4 tablespoons margarine or
    butter
1 package dry yeast
¼ cup warm, not hot, water

1 egg, well beaten
1⅓ cups sifted all-purpose flour
1½ cups canned apples, sliced,
    drained
2 tablespoons brown sugar
¼ teaspoon ground cinnamon
¼ teaspoon ground nutmeg

Scald milk. Stir in sugar, salt, and 2 tablespoons of margarine. Cool to lukewarm. Dissolve yeast in warm water. Stir in lukewarm milk mixture. Add egg and flour. Beat until smooth. Spread dough evenly in greased 9- x 9- x 2-inch pan. Arrange apple slices on top. Sprinkle with mixture of brown sugar, cinnamon, and nutmeg. Dot with remaining margarine. Cover and let rise in warm place, free from draft, until doubled in bulk, about 40 minutes. Bake at 400° for 25 minutes.

❦ Fresh Apple Cake
(tube pan)

1¼ cups corn oil
2 cups sugar
3 cups all-purpose flour
3 eggs
2 teaspoons vanilla extract
1 teaspoon salt

1 teaspoon soda
2 cups chopped fresh apples
1 cup chopped nuts
1 (3½-ounce) can flaked
    coconut

Mix corn oil and sugar together with spoon until sugar is dissolved. Combine dry ingredients and add to sugar mixture alternately with eggs, beating after each addition.

Add vanilla, chopped apples, nuts, and coconut. Batter will be very thick. Put into greased and floured tube pan. Bake at 350° for 1¼ hours. Cool in pan.

❦ Apple Dapple Cake
(8- OR 9-INCH TUBE PAN)

3 eggs	1 teaspoon soda
1½ cups salad oil	2 teaspoons vanilla extract
2 cups sugar	3 cups chopped apples
3 cups all-purpose flour	1½ cups chopped pecans
1 teaspoon salt	

Mix eggs, salad oil, and sugar, and blend well. Add flour, salt, and soda mixed well. Add vanilla, chopped apples, and nuts. Put into greased 8- or 9-inch tube pan. Bake at 350° for 1 hour. While cake is still hot, pour hot topping over it in the pan and let cool. When completely cold, remove from pan.

Topping

1 cup brown sugar	1 stick margarine
¼ cup milk	

Combine all ingredients and cook 2½ minutes. Pour hot over cake in pan. Let set until cold.

❦ All-Purpose Fresh Apple Cake
(10-INCH TUBE PAN)

2½ cups all-purpose flour	4 eggs
1 teaspoon ground cinnamon	½ cup water
1 teaspoon ground allspice	3 medium apples, chopped
1 teaspoon soda	1 cup pecans, finely chopped
1 cup butter or margarine	1 teaspoon vanilla extract
2 cups sugar	

Combine flour, spices, and soda. Cream butter or margarine and sugar using medium speed on mixer. Add eggs, one at a time, beating well after each addition. Add dry ingredients to creamed mixture alternately with water. Add chopped apples and nuts and fold into mixture. Add vanilla. Pour into greased tube pan lined with waxed paper. Bake at 350° for 1½ hours; or bake in three 8-inch layer pans at 400° for 30 minutes.

❦ Apple-Date Cake

(TUBE PAN)

2 cups sugar	3 cups all-purpose flour
1½ cups cooking oil	1¼ teaspoons soda
2 teaspoons vanilla extract	2 cups peeled and chopped,
2 eggs, well beaten	fresh tart apples
Juice of ½ lemon	1 cup chopped dates
1 teaspoon salt	1½ to 2 cups chopped pecans

Combine sugar, oil, vanilla, eggs, lemon juice, and salt in a mixing bowl. Beat well. Mix flour and soda. Add to first mixture and beat well again. Add apples, dates, and pecans. Mix well. Bake in a tube pan which has been greased and dusted with flour. Bake at 325° for 1½ hours.

Note: Batter will be very thick and you may need to mix apples, dates, and pecans with hands.

❦ Applesauce Cake

(9-INCH TUBE PAN)

½ cup shortening	½ teaspoon salt
1 cup sugar	1 teaspoon soda
1 egg	½ teaspoon ground cinnamon
1¾ cups all-purpose flour	¼ teaspoon ground cloves
1 cup raisins	1 cup applesauce
1 cup finely chopped nuts	

Cream shortening and sugar well; add egg and beat until light and fluffy. Sprinkle 2 tablespoons flour over the combined raisins and nuts. Combine remaining flour with salt, soda, cinnamon, and cloves. Heat applesauce and add to creamed mixture alternately with the dry ingredients, mixing only until well blended. Stir in raisins and nuts. Pour into a greased and floured 9-inch tube pan. Bake at 350° for 40 minutes. Cool thoroughly.

❦ Applesauce Layer Cake

(THREE 8- OR 9-INCH LAYER PANS)

⅔ cup butter
2 cups sugar
4 egg yolks
¾ cup unsweetened
  applesauce
2½ cups all-purpose flour
3 teaspoons baking powder
1 teaspoon ground cloves
1 teaspoon ground cinnamon

½ teaspoon ground nutmeg
½ teaspoon ground allspice
2 tablespoons cocoa
½ cup milk
2 teaspoons vanilla extract
⅔ cup chopped pecans or
  walnuts
⅔ cup seedless raisins
4 egg whites

Cream butter; add sugar and beat until well blended. Add beaten yolks and applesauce and beat until mixture is smooth. Combine flour with baking powder, spices, and cocoa. Add to creamed mixture alternately with milk. When well mixed, add vanilla, nuts, and raisins. Fold in stiffly beaten egg whites. Turn into three 8- or 9-inch layer cake pans and bake at 350° for about 40 minutes. Put together with Caramel Frosting.

❦ Easy Applesauce Cake

(13- x 9- x 2-INCH PAN)

2½ cups all-purpose flour
2 cups sugar
1½ teaspoons soda
1½ teaspoons salt
¼ teaspoon baking powder
¾ teaspoon ground cinnamon
½ teaspoon ground cloves
½ teaspoon ground allspice

½ cup soft shortening
½ cup water
1½ cups canned applesauce
2 eggs
½ cup chopped walnuts or
  pecans
1 cup raisins

Measure all ingredients into large mixing bowl. Blend for 30 seconds at lowest speed on electric mixer, then for 3 minutes at medium speed, scraping bowl often. Pour into greased and floured pan 13 x 9 x 2 inches. Bake at 350° for 60 to 65 minutes, or until cake tests done with wooden pick. Frost with Browned Butter Frosting, if desired.

❦ Applesauce-Nut Cake

(13- x 9- x 2-inch pan)

¾ cup butter
1 cup granulated sugar
1 cup brown sugar
3 eggs
3 cups applesauce
3½ cups all-purpose flour
2 teaspoons baking powder

1 teaspoon salt
¾ teaspoon ground cloves
1 teaspoon ground nutmeg
3 teaspoons ground cinnamon
1 pound seedless raisins
1½ cups chopped pecans

Cream butter and sugar. Add eggs and applesauce and beat well. Combine dry ingredients and stir in. Add raisins and pecans and mix well. Pour into greased 13- x 9- x 2-inch cake pan. Bake at 325° for 2 hours.

❦ Banana-Nut Loaf

(9- or 10-inch tube pan)

½ cup butter or margarine
2 cups sugar
2 eggs
2 cups mashed bananas
3 cups all-purpose flour

½ teaspoon salt
1½ teaspoons soda
½ cup buttermilk
½ cup chopped nuts

Cream butter and sugar. Add eggs and beat until smooth. Add bananas. Combine flour and salt. Dissolve soda in buttermilk. Add dry mixture to creamed mixture alternately with buttermilk. Pour batter in greased 9- or 10-inch tube pan. Bake at 350° for 1 hour.

❦ Fiesta Banana Cake

(two 8- or 9-inch layer pans)

½ cup shortening
1½ cups sugar
2 eggs, unbeaten
½ cup sour milk or buttermilk
1 cup mashed bananas

2 cups cake flour
1 teaspoon baking powder
1 teaspoon soda
¾ teaspoon salt
½ cup chopped pecans

Cream shortening and sugar together until smooth. Add eggs, milk, and bananas; mix well. Add dry ingredients and beat for 2 minutes. Add nuts. Put batter into two greased 8- or 9-inch square cake pans. Bake at 375° for 25 minutes, or until done. Cool and frost with Speedy Banana Frosting.

❧ Sour Cream–Banana Cake

(TWO 8-INCH LAYER PANS)

1 stick butter or margarine	1 teaspoon soda
1 cup sugar	1 cup commercial sour cream
2 eggs	1 teaspoon vanilla extract
2 cups all-purpose flour	2 medium (very ripe)
1 teaspoon baking powder	bananas, mashed

Cream butter and sugar until smooth. Add eggs, one at a time, beating well after each addition. Combine dry ingredients and add to creamed mixture alternately with sour cream. Add vanilla, and fold in mashed bananas. Put batter into two greased 8-inch cake pans. Bake at 350° about 25 to 30 minutes. When cool, frost with a chocolate frosting.

❧ Banana-Nut Spice Cake

(THREE LOAF PANS)

6 very ripe bananas	2 teaspoons soda
½ cup vegetable oil	2½ teaspoons ground cinnamon
¼ pound butter	1½ teaspoons ground cloves
2 cups sugar	½ teaspoon salt
4 eggs	1½ cups seedless raisins
3 cups all-purpose flour	1½ cups chopped pecans

Mash bananas; pour vegetable oil over bananas and let stand while mixing cake. Cream butter and sugar; add eggs, one at a time, beating well after each addition. Stir in banana mixture and mix well. Add dry ingredients, which have been combined. Stir in raisins and pecans and mix thoroughly. Spoon mixture into three greased loaf pans and bake at 250° for 1½ hours.

❧ Banana-Nut Cake

(LARGE TUBE PAN)

1 cup soft vegetable shortening	6 tablespoons buttermilk
2½ cups sugar	2 teaspoons vanilla extract
3 cups all-purpose flour	2 cups mashed ripe bananas
1½ teaspoons soda	1 cup chopped pecans
1 teaspoon salt	4 egg whites, beaten
4 egg yolks, beaten	

Cream shortening and sugar. Combine dry ingredients and add to creamed mixture alternately with beaten egg yolks and buttermilk. Add vanilla, mashed bananas, and pecans. Fold in beaten egg whites. Bake in large greased tube pan at 325° for about 1½ hours.

❧ Banana-Nut Layer Cake

(TWO 8-INCH LAYER PANS)

½ cup shortening	2 cups all-purpose flour
1½ cups sugar	1 teaspoon baking powder
2 eggs	½ teaspoon salt
1 cup mashed bananas	½ teaspoon soda
⅓ cup buttermilk	¾ cup chopped nuts
1 teaspoon vanilla extract	

Cream shortening, add sugar, and blend well. Add eggs, one at a time, beating well. Add bananas and beat for 1 minute. Combine buttermilk and vanilla. Sift together flour, baking powder, salt, and soda. Add to creamed mixture alternately with milk mixture, ending with flour mixture. Mix well between additions. Stir in nuts and pour into two greased and floured 8-inch cake pans. Bake at 350° for 35 to 40 minutes. Frost with a caramel frosting.

❧ Banana Layer Cake No. 1

(TWO 9-INCH LAYER PANS)

2½ cups cake flour
1 teaspoon soda
½ teaspoon baking powder
½ teaspoon salt
¾ cup butter or shortening
1½ cups sugar

2 eggs
¼ cup sour milk or buttermilk
1 teaspoon vanilla extract
1¼ cups ripe bananas (forced through food mill, then measured)

Sift flour once, then measure; sift again with soda, baking powder, and salt. Cream butter, add sugar, and cream together until light and fluffy. Add the whole eggs, beating well after each addition. Add sour milk and vanilla to bananas. Add alternately the flour and banana mixtures to butter mixture, beginning and ending with the dry ingredients. Beat until smooth and well blended. Do not overmix. Divide evenly into two 9-inch layer cake pans, greased and dusted lightly with flour. Bake at 375° for 25 to 30 minutes. Frost with Butter Frosting, or as desired.

❧ Banana Layer Cake No. 2

(TWO 8- OR 9-INCH LAYER PANS)

1 cup shortening
2 cups sugar
2 eggs
2 cups mashed ripe bananas
3 cups cake flour

1 teaspoon salt
1 teaspoon soda
¼ cup buttermilk
1 teaspoon vanilla extract
1 cup chopped pecans

Cream shortening and sugar until light and fluffy. Add eggs one at a time, beating well after each addition. Add mashed bananas and mix well. Combine dry ingredients. Add soda to buttermilk and add to creamed mixture alternately with dry ingredients, beginning and ending with dry ingredients. Stir in vanilla and nuts.

Put in two greased 8- or 9-inch layer cake pans and bake at 350° for 40 to 50 minutes, or until cake tests done.

❧ Butterscotch Layer Cake

(TWO 8- OR 9-INCH LAYER PANS)

1 (6-ounce) package butterscotch pieces	1 cup brown sugar
2½ cups all-purpose flour	⅔ cup milk
3 teaspoons baking powder	⅓ cup soft butter or margarine
1½ teaspoons salt	½ teaspoon vanilla extract
½ teaspoon soda	⅓ cup milk
	3 eggs

Melt butterscotch pieces over hot (not boiling) water. Cool. Sift together in a large bowl the flour, baking powder, salt, and soda. Add brown sugar, ⅔ cup milk, soft butter, and vanilla. Mix till blended. Beat 2 minutes by hand or at low speed on electric mixer. Add melted butterscotch, ⅓ cup milk, and 3 eggs; beat an additional 2 minutes. Pour batter into two lightly greased and floured 8- or 9-inch layer pans. Bake at 375° for 20 to 25 minutes. Let cool on cake rack 10 minutes. Remove from pans and cool throughly. Frost with Butterscotch Delight Frosting.

❧ Mardi Gras Cake

(TWO 9-INCH LAYER PANS)

⅔ cup butterscotch pieces	1 cup sugar
¼ cup water	¼ cup brown sugar, firmly packed
2¼ cups all-purpose flour	½ cup shortening
1 teaspoon salt	3 eggs, unbeaten
1 teaspoon soda	1 cup buttermilk
½ teaspoon baking powder	

Melt butterscotch pieces in water in saucepan. Cool. Combine flour with salt, soda, and baking powder; set aside. Add sugar and brown sugar gradually to shortening, creaming well. Blend in eggs, beating well after each addition. Add butterscotch pieces; mix well. Add dry ingredients alternately with buttermilk, beginning and ending with dry ingredients. Blend well after each addition. (With mixer, use a low speed.) Put batter in two 9-inch greased and floured round layer pans. Bake at 375° for 30 to 35 minutes. Cool; spread Mardi Gras Filling between layers and on top to within ½ inch of edge. Frost sides and top edge with Seafoam Frosting or whipped cream.

❦ Carrot Loaf Cake

(TWO LARGE OR THREE SMALL LOAF PANS)

2 cups sugar
3 cups all-purpose flour
1 teaspoon soda
½ teaspoon salt
1 teaspoon ground cinnamon
2 cups coarsely grated carrots
1⅓ cups salad oil

2 eggs, beaten
1 cup chopped nuts
1 cup crushed pineapple, drained
1 teaspoon vanilla extract
1 teaspoon lemon extract
½ teaspoon almond extract

Combine dry ingredients in large mixing bowl. Add carrots, salad oil, and eggs. Beat until well mixed. Add other ingredients and stir. Put batter in two large or three small loaf pans which have been oiled and floured. Bake at 350° for 1 hour.

❦ Carrot Sheet Cake

(13- x 9- x 2-INCH PAN)

2 cups all-purpose flour
2½ cups sugar
2 teaspoons soda
½ teaspoon salt
2 teaspoons ground cinnamon
3 eggs
1 cup salad oil

1 teaspoon vanilla extract
1 cup chopped dates
1 cup chopped nuts
2 cups grated raw carrots
1 cup crushed pineapple (drained)

Sift dry ingredients together. Make a well in the center of dry ingredients and add eggs, cooking oil, and vanilla. Mix together and add dates, nuts, carrots, and pineapple. (Mixture will be very stiff at first, but will get thinner after the carrots are added.) Grease a 13- x 9- x 2-inch pan and line with waxed paper. Bake at 350° for 1 hour. No frosting is necessary.

Note: 1 cup candied fruits may be substituted for 1 cup chopped dates.

❧ Carrot Layer Cake

(THREE 9-INCH LAYER PANS)

2 cups sugar	2 teaspoons baking powder
1½ cups salad oil	2 teaspoons ground cinnamon
4 eggs, well beaten	1 teaspoon salt
2 teaspoons soda	1 cup chopped pecans
2 cups all-purpose flour	3 cups grated carrots

Mix sugar and salad oil together. Add well-beaten eggs and mix well. Combine dry ingredients and stir in. Mix until smooth. Add chopped pecans and grated carrots. Bake in three greased 9-inch layer cake pans at 325° about 30 minutes. Frost with Frosting for Carrot Cake.

❧ Party Cheesecake

(9-INCH SPRINGFORM PAN)

1 cup fine cornflake crumbs	3 cups creamed cottage cheese
¼ cup soft butter or margarine	Grated rind and juice of 2
1¼ cups sugar	lemons
3 envelopes unflavored	1 cup heavy cream
gelatin	4 egg whites, beaten
4 egg yolks	Sweetened halved
¾ teaspoon salt	strawberries and pineapple
1½ cups milk	tidbits

Mix crumbs, butter, and ¼ cup sugar. Press firmly on bottom of 9-inch springform or loose-bottomed pan; chill. In top part of double boiler combine 1 cup sugar and gelatin. Add egg yolks, salt, and milk; beat with rotary beater until blended. Cook over simmering water, stirring, until slightly thickened. Cool. Force cottage cheese through food mill or sieve. Beat into cooked mixture with lemon rind and juice. Whip cream until stiff and fold with stiffly beaten egg whites into mixture. Pour into prepared pan and chill until firm. Remove sides of pan and place on serving dish. Decorate with strawberry halves and pineapple tidbits.

Note: Cheesecake needs to be kept refrigerated at all times. Do not make too far in advance of serving or it will lose its fluffiness.

℘ Creamy Cheesecake

(8-INCH LAYER PAN)

1¼ cups fine graham cracker crumbs
½ cup brown sugar
½ teaspoon ground cinnamon
⅓ cup melted butter or margarine
1 (8-ounce) package cream cheese

1 cup creamy cottage cheese
½ cup sugar
2 tablespoons all-purpose flour
¼ teaspoon salt
1 teaspoon vanilla extract
4 eggs, separated
1 cup light cream

Mix crumbs, brown sugar, cinnamon, and butter or margarine. Press in even layer over bottom and sides of an 8-inch square cake pan.

Soften cream cheese. Press cottage cheese through a sieve and mix with the cream cheese. Mix the sugar, flour, and salt; cream thoroughly with the two cheeses. Add the vanilla. Add egg yolks, one at a time, beating well after each addition. Add the cream and mix well. Fold in the beaten egg whites. Pour this mixture on top of the crumbs. Bake at 325° about 1 hour. Yield: 8 servings.

℘ Cheesecake No. 1

(SPRINGFORM PAN)

1 cup graham cracker or cornflake crumbs
¼ cup sugar
1 teaspoon ground cinnamon
½ cup soft butter or margarine
½ pound cream cheese
1 cup creamed cottage cheese

2 eggs
1 cup sugar
2 tablespoons cornstarch
Pinch of salt
1 cup commercial sour cream
¾ cup milk
1 teaspoon vanilla extract

Blend crumbs with sugar and cinnamon. Work in soft butter. Line a well-buttered springform pan with the mixture; reserve ¼ cup. Chill.

Beat cream cheese and cottage cheese until smooth. Add eggs, beating well after each addition. Stir in sugar, cornstarch, and salt. Add sour cream, milk, and vanilla gradually. This makes a thin batter. Pour the batter carefully into the crumb-lined pan and sprinkle with reserved crumbs. Bake at 350° for 1 hour. Turn off the heat and cool cake in oven for 1 hour.

❧ Cheesecake No. 2

(9-INCH SPRINGFORM PAN)

1¼ cups graham cracker crumbs
2 tablespoons sugar
¼ cup melted butter or
   margarine
1 pound cream cheese
1 cup sugar
2 tablespoons all-purpose
   flour

½ teaspoon salt
4 egg yolks, beaten
1 teaspoon vanilla extract
1 cup whipping cream
4 egg whites, beaten

Mix crumbs, 2 tablespoons sugar, and butter. Press firmly on bottom of 9-inch springform pan. Cream cheese until consistency of whipped cream. Gradually add sugar, mixing until light and spongy. Add flour mixed with salt. Add egg yolks and vanilla; mix lightly. Add cream. Fold in egg whites. Pour gently on top of crumb crust. Bake at 325° for 1 hour.

Glaze

Drain 1 (10-ounce) package thawed, frozen strawberries and save syrup. Measure syrup, adding water if needed to make ⅔ cup. Mix in saucepan: 2 tablespoons cornstarch, 2 tablespoons sugar, 2 tablespoons lemon juice. Stir in strawberry syrup. Mix until smooth. Cook over medium heat, stirring until thick and clear. Cool slightly. Stir in strawberries. Spread over cheesecake.

❧ Cheesecake No. 3

(13- x 9- x 2-INCH CAKE PAN)

1½ envelopes unflavored gelatin
1 cup cold water
½ cup sugar
½ cup cold water
4 egg yolks
4 (3-ounce) packages cream
   cheese, softened

2½ tablespoons lemon juice
   (fresh)
8 or 10 graham crackers
¼ cup sugar
4 tablespoons butter
1 cup whipping cream
4 egg whites

Sprinkle gelatin in 1 cup cold water to which sugar has been added; put in top of double boiler. Haven't got one? OK, put the ingredients in a medium-sized pan and put that into a larger pan that has about an inch of water in it. Turn on the heat and stir until the gelatin dissolves. In small bowl put ½ cup of cold water and add 4 egg yolks; mix well with a beater. Add this to gelatin mixture and stir until all is blended and somewhat thickened. Remove from heat.

Take the cream cheese and 2½ tablespoons lemon juice, and mix until creamy. If you have an electric beater you're way ahead of the game. Now blend this cheese mixture into the gelatin mixture; when it is well blended and smooth, put it into the refrigerator. Watch it, for you want it to thicken but not set. Leave just half an hour or so.

While you're waiting, you might as well be doing something constructive, so take those graham crackers and crush them into fine crumbs; then mix them with ¼ cup sugar and 4 tablespoons butter, which you have, I hope, allowed to soften. Mix this well and line the bottom and sides of a 13- x 9- x 2-inch rectangular cake pan. Use only about half of the crumb mixture; you'll need the rest later.

Now whip the cream, take the cooled mixture from the refrigerator, and blend the cream into the mixture; take those 4 egg whites that you had left over, beat until stiff, and fold into the cake filling. Looks like enough for an army, doesn't it? Never fear. Pour all into the pan. Take the remaining crumb mixture and sprinkle thickly over the top of the cake. Return it to the refrigerator for 3 to 4 hours to set.

❦ Sweet Potato Cheesecake

(9-INCH PIE PLATE)

1 cup commercial sour cream
¾ cup cooked mashed sweet
    potatoes (cold)
3 tablespoons baby food
    apricots
1 tablespoon lemon juice
½ teaspoon vanilla extract

⅛ teaspoon ground mace
⅓ cup milk
1 (10¾-ounce) package
    cheesecake mix
1 (9-inch) prepared graham
    cracker crust

Combine sour cream, sweet potatoes, apricots, lemon juice, vanilla, mace, and milk and blend thoroughly. Add cheesecake mix and beat 3 minutes until the mixture thickens. Spoon into the graham cracker crust and bake at 400° for 8 minutes; chill in refrigerator for 2 hours before serving. Yield: 6 servings.

❦ Tangy Lemon Cheesecake

(8-INCH SPRINGFORM PAN)

2 tablespoons unflavored gelatin	2 tablespoons lemon juice
1 cup sugar	½ cup graham cracker crumbs
¼ teaspoon salt	¼ teaspoon ground cinnamon
2 egg yolks	½ teaspoon grated lemon rind
¾ cup milk	1 tablespoon sugar
3 cups cottage cheese, beaten until almost smooth	2 tablespoons melted butter
2 tablespoons grated lemon rind	2 egg whites
	1 cup cream, whipped

Mix gelatin, 1 cup sugar, and salt in top of double boiler. Beat together egg yolks and milk; stir into gelatin mixture. Cook over boiling water, stirring constantly, about 10 minutes, or until gelatin is dissolved and mixture is slightly thickened. Remove from heat. Mix cottage cheese, 2 tablespoons lemon rind, and lemon juice. Gradually add and stir in gelatin mixture. Mix until blended. Chill, stirring occasionally, until mixture mounds slightly when dropped from spoon.

Mix graham cracker crumbs, cinnamon, ½ teaspoon lemon rind, 1 tablespoon sugar, and butter; reserve as topping for cake.

Beat egg whites until stiff, but not dry. Gently fold with whipped cream into cheese mixture. Pour into 8-inch springform pan and sprinkle top with crumbs. Chill until firm. Garnish with pineapple and maraschino cherries.

❦ Prize Chocolate Cake

(TWO 8-INCH LAYER PANS)

4 squares unsweetened chocolate	1 cup all-purpose flour
1 cup milk	1 teaspoon baking powder
4 egg yolks	1 teaspoon vanilla extract
1¾ cups sugar	

Heat chocolate in milk over low heat until chocolate melts. Do not let milk boil. Cool. Beat egg yolks and sugar together. Add chocolate mixture; then flour and baking powder which have been sifted together. Add vanilla. Fold in stiffly beaten egg whites. Bake in two greased 8-inch layer cake pans at 350° for 20 to 25 minutes. Frost as desired.

❦ Brown Beauty Cake

(TWO 9-INCH LAYER PANS)

⅓ cup semi-sweet chocolate pieces
⅓ cup butterscotch pieces
¼ cup water
½ cup shortening
1¼ cups sugar
3 eggs

2¼ cups sifted all-purpose flour
1 teaspoon salt
½ teaspoon baking powder
1 teaspoon soda
1 cup buttermilk

Combine chocolate and butterscotch pieces with water; heat until melted. Cool. Combine shortening and sugar and beat until creamy. Beat in eggs, one at a time. Blend in chocolate-butterscotch mixture. Sift flour with salt, baking powder, and soda; add alternately with buttermilk. Pour into two greased and floured 9-inch square or round layer cakes pans. Bake at 375° for 25 to 30 minutes. Remove from pans. When cold, spread with Brown Beauty Frosting.

❦ Chocolate Cream Cake

(THREE 9-INCH LAYER PANS)

1 (8-ounce) package cream cheese,
   softened
1 (3-ounce) package cream
   cheese, softened
2 sticks butter
2 (1-pound) boxes powdered
   sugar
1 (4-ounce) package sweet
   chocolate

¼ cup water
¼ cup shortening
3 eggs
2¼ cups all-purpose flour
1 teaspoon soda
1 teaspoon salt
1 cup buttermilk
1 teaspoon vanilla extract

Put cream cheese and butter in large mixing bowl. Beat until light and fluffy. Stir in powdered sugar gradually and beat well. Melt chocolate in water in top of a double boiler, and stir into sugar mixture.

Divide sugar mixture into two parts. Reserve one part for the frosting. To the other half add shortening and eggs and beat well. Combine flour, soda, and salt, and add to egg-sugar mixture alternately with buttermilk. Stir in vanilla and mix well. Spoon batter evenly into three greased 9-inch layer cake pans and bake at 350° for 35 minutes or until cake tests done. After cake has cooled, put layers together with reserved sugar mixture.

❧ Sweet Chocolate Cake

(THREE 8- OR 9-INCH LAYER PANS)

1 cup shortening	2½ cups cake flour
2 cups sugar	½ teaspoon salt
4 egg yolks	1 teaspoon soda
1 (¼-pound) package sweet	1 cup buttermilk
cooking chocolate	4 egg whites, stiffly beaten
½ cup boiling water	1 teaspoon vanilla extract

Cream shortening; add sugar, then egg yolks one at a time. Add chocolate melted in boiling water, then cooled. Mix well. Combine dry ingredients. Add alternately with milk to creamed mixture. Beat egg whites stiff and fold in. Add vanilla. Bake in three greased 8- or 9-inch layer cake pans at 350° for about 40 minutes.

❧ Scotch Cake

(13- x 9- x 2-INCH PAN)

2 cups all-purpose flour	½ cup buttermilk
2 cups sugar	2 eggs
1 stick margarine	1 teaspoon soda
½ cup vegetable shortening	1 teaspoon ground cinnamon
4 tablespoons cocoa	1 teaspoon vanilla extract
1 cup water	

Combine flour and sugar in large mixing bowl. In a saucepan put margarine, shortening, cocoa, and water; bring to a rapid boil and then pour into flour and sugar mixture. Mix well. Add other ingredients and mix well. Put into a greased 13- x 9- x 2-inch pan and bake at 400° for 30 minutes. Start making frosting 5 minutes before cake has finished baking.

Frosting for Scotch Cake

1 stick margarine	1 teaspoon vanilla extract
4 tablespoons cocoa	1 cup chopped peanuts
6 tablespoons milk	1 cup flaked coconut
1 box powdered sugar	

Bring to a boil the margarine, cocoa, and milk, stirring constantly to keep from burning. Remove from heat; add other ingredients. Spread on hot cake.

❦ Chocolate-Pineapple Cake

(THREE 9-INCH LAYER PANS)

1 cup butter
2½ cups sugar
5 egg yolks
2 squares melted chocolate
Grated rind of 1 orange
½ cup orange juice

1 teaspoon vanilla extract
3 cups cake flour
1 cup buttermilk
1 teaspoon soda
5 egg whites, stiffly beaten

Cream butter and add sugar. Mix well. Add beaten egg yolks and mix well. Add melted chocolate and grated orange rind, orange juice, and vanilla. Alternately add the flour and buttermilk, adding the soda to the last portion of the milk before putting into batter. Mix well. Fold in stiffly beaten egg whites. Pour into three 9-inch cake pans that have been greased and waxed paper placed in the bottoms. Bake at 350° about 30 minutes or until loosened around edges. Spread Pineapple Filling between layers. Frost top and sides as desired.

❦ White Chocolate Cake

(THREE 9-INCH LAYER PANS)

⅓ cup white chocolate, cut in
   small pieces
½ cup hot water
1 cup butter
1½ cups sugar
4 egg yolks, unbeaten

1 teaspoon vanilla extract
2½ cups sifted cake flour
1 teaspoon baking soda
1 cup buttermilk
4 egg whites, stiffly beaten

Melt white chocolate in hot water; allow to cool. Cream butter and sugar together until light and fluffy. Add egg yolks, one at a time, beating well after each addition. Add melted white chocolate and vanilla.

Sift flour and baking soda together and add alternately with buttermilk to creamed mixture. Gently fold in stiffly beaten egg whites. Pour into three greased and floured 9-inch layer pans. Bake 30 to 35 minutes in a 350° oven. Cool. Frost with White Chocolate Frosting.

❦ Red Earth Cake

(TWO 8-INCH LAYER PANS)

½ cup shortening
1½ cups sugar
1 egg, well beaten
4 tablespoons cocoa
1 teaspoon red food coloring
2 tablespoons hot coffee

1¾ cups all-purpose flour
1 teaspoon salt
1 teaspoon soda
1 cup buttermilk
1 teaspoon vanilla extract

Cream shortening and sugar. Add egg and blend. Mix cocoa, coloring, and hot coffee to smooth paste. Stir into creamed mixture. Combine flour with salt and soda. Add to creamed mixture alternately with buttermilk, beating after each addition. Add vanilla.

Turn into two 8-inch cake pans, lined on bottoms with oiled waxed paper, or a 13- x 9-inch pan. Bake at 375° for 30 to 35 minutes. Frost with Mocha Frosting.

❦ Chocolate Yeast Cake

(TWO LAYER PANS)

½ package yeast
3 tablespoons very warm
   water
1⅓ cups plus ½ teaspoon sugar
½ cup butter
½ teaspoon salt
2 eggs, well beaten

½ cup cocoa
⅔ cup sweet milk
1 teaspoon vanilla extract
2 cups all-purpose flour
¾ teaspoon baking soda
2 tablespoons warm water

Stir yeast in 3 tablespoons lukewarm water. Add ½ teaspoon sugar. Let stand for 5 minutes. Cream butter, 1 cup sugar, and salt. Add eggs and then add cocoa mixed with ⅓ cup sugar. Stir in milk, vanilla, and flour alternately. Add softened yeast; mix well. Cover batter; let stand in a cool place overnight.

Dissolve soda in 2 tablespoons warm water; stir into batter. Pour in two greased layer cake pans. Bake at once in 350° oven about 25 minutes or until cake tests done. Frost cake with your favorite white frosting.

♋ Chip-Nut Cocoa Cake

(13- x 9- x 2-INCH PAN)

1 cup finely chopped dates	1 teaspoon soda
1 cup boiling water	1¾ cups sifted all-purpose flour
¼ cup cocoa	1 teaspoon vanilla extract
½ teaspoon salt	½ cup chopped nuts (optional)
1 cup shortening	1 cup (6-ounce package)
1 cup sugar	chocolate pieces
2 eggs, beaten	

Mix together dates, water, and soda. Cool. Sift flour, cocoa, and salt together. Cream shortening thoroughly. Add sugar gradually and cream together until light and fluffy. Add the eggs and vanilla; beat well. Then add flour alternately with the date mixture, beating after each addition. Pour batter into a 13- x 9- x 2-inch pan which has been greased on the bottom. Sprinkle nuts and pieces over top and press lightly into batter. Bake at 350° for 40 to 45 minutes. Cool and cut in bars. Yield: 3 dozen.

♋ Chocolate-Date Cake

(9-INCH TUBE PAN)

1½ cups all-purpose flour	2 cups sifted sugar
½ pound pitted dates	4 egg yolks
3 teaspoons baking powder	½ teaspoon vanilla extract
¼ teaspoon salt	1 tablespoon orange rind,
3½ ounces bitter chocolate,	grated
melted	½ cup chopped walnuts
1 cup milk	4 egg whites, beaten

Measure flour; sprinkle 2 tablespoons on waxed paper. With scissors, cut dates as fine as possible onto flour. Mix together. Reserve. Mix together remainder of flour, baking powder, and salt. Reserve. Melt chocolate and milk in double boiler over hot water. Add 1 cup sugar and stir until smooth. Reserve. Beat egg yolks in mixing bowl until light colored. Gradually beat in remaining cup sugar until well blended. Stir in chocolate mixture. Stir in vanilla and sifted ingredients until well blended. Stir in dates, orange rind, and walnuts. Beat egg whites until stiff; fold into mixture. Pour into ungreased 9-inch tube pan. Bake at 350° for 1 hour and 10 minutes. Cool in pan.

❦ Brownstone Front Cake

(TUBE PAN)

2 sticks margarine	1 cup buttermilk
2 cups sugar	1 teaspoon vanilla extract
3 eggs	3 cups all-purpose flour
1 ounce unsweetened chocolate, melted in 2 tablespoons water	1 teaspoon soda

Cream margarine and sugar; add eggs, and cream until light. Add cooled chocolate mixture. Add milk and vanilla alternately with sifted flour and soda. Bake in greased tube pan at 325° for 1 hour and 15 minutes. Let cool, remove from pan, and cover with frosting, if desired.

❦ Peanut Butter-Chocolate Cake

(TWO 8-INCH LAYER PANS)

1¾ cups sifted cake flour	3 tablespoons peanut butter
¾ teaspoon soda	1 cup milk
¾ teaspoon salt	1 teaspoon vanilla extract
1 cup sugar	2 squares unsweetened chocolate, melted
2 tablespoons shortening	

Sift flour once, measure; add soda, salt, and sugar and sift together three times. Cream shortening and peanut butter until well blended. Then add sifted dry ingredients, milk, and vanilla. Stir in unsweetened chocolate. Stir until all flour is dampened. Beat vigorously 1 minute. Turn into two 8-inch layer pans which have been greased, lined with waxed paper, and greased again. Bake at 350° for 30 minutes or until done.

❦ Red Cake

(THREE 9-INCH LAYER PANS)

½ cup vegetable shortening	1 scant teaspoon salt
1½ cups sugar	1 teaspoon soda
2 eggs	2½ cups cake flour
1½ ounces red food coloring	1 cup buttermilk
2 level tablespoons cocoa	2 tablespoons vanilla extract

Cream the shortening and sugar; add the eggs, and cream until well blended. Mix the food coloring and cocoa and add to the creamed mixture. Sift salt, soda, and cake flour. Add dry ingredients and liquids alternately to creamed mixture. Fold; do not beat. Bake in three greased 9-inch cake pans at 350° for 30 to 35 minutes. Serve as a three-layer cake, frosted with your favorite white frosting.

❦ Coffee-Chocolate Cake

(TWO 9-INCH LAYER PANS)

1 cup butter or margarine	1 teaspoon ground nutmeg
2 cups sugar	1 teaspoon ground allspice
4 eggs	1 teaspoon ground cloves
½ cup cocoa	½ teaspoon soda
2 cups sifted all-purpose flour	1 cup cold coffee
1 teaspoon ground cinnamon	1 tablespoon vanilla extract

Cream butter and sugar. Add eggs, one at a time, beating after each addition until smooth. Mix cocoa, flour, and spices; dissolve soda in coffee, and add dry ingredients to creamed mixture alternately with the coffee. Mix well. Add vanilla. Pour into two greased and floured 9-inch cake pans. Bake at 350° for 35 to 40 minutes. Frost as desired.

❦ Chocolate Fudge Cake

(THREE 9-INCH LAYER PANS)

2¼ cups all-purpose flour	1 teaspoon vanilla extract
1 teaspoon soda	2 eggs, well beaten
1 teaspoon baking powder	1 cup sour milk
¾ teaspoon salt	½ cup cocoa
½ cup shortening	⅓ cup hot water
1½ cups sugar	

Combine flour, soda, baking powder, and salt. Cream shortening; add sugar gradually and beat after each addition. Add vanilla, then well-beaten eggs; beat in flour mixture alternately with milk. Mix cocoa and hot water to form a smooth paste; beat into batter. Put into three greased 9-inch layer cake pans (or two, if you like thick layers). Bake at 350° for 20 to 25 minutes. Cool, and frost as desired.

❧ Georgia Fudge Cake
(TWO 8-INCH LAYER PANS)

2 cups sifted cake flour	1 teaspoon vanilla extract
½ teaspoon salt	2 squares unsweetened
1 teaspoon soda	chocolate, melted and
½ cup shortening	cooled
1½ cups sugar	1 cup commercial sour cream
2 eggs, separated	

Sift the flour, salt, and soda together. Cream shortening and add the sugar gradually, beating until light. Beat the egg yolks and whites separately. Add egg yolks and vanilla to creamed mixture. Stir in the melted chocolate. Add sifted dry ingredients alternately with sour cream, beating after each addition. Fold in stiffly beaten egg whites. Bake in two 8-inch layer pans at 350° about 25 or 30 minutes. Frost as desired.

❧ Marshmallow-Chocolate Cake
(TWO 8-INCH LAYER PANS)

1 (¼-pound) package	1 teaspoon salt
marshmallows	2 eggs, beaten
2 squares unsweetened	1 cup sugar
chocolate, grated	1 cup commercial sour cream
½ cup hot water	1 teaspoon vanilla extract
1½ cups all-purpose flour	
1 teaspoon soda	

Melt marshmallows and chocolate over water, add hot water, beating to smooth paste, cool. Combine flour, soda, and salt. Beat eggs, add sugar, and whip until creamy. Add sour cream and stir until smooth; fold flour mixture gradually into egg mixture. Carefully fold in chocolate-marshmallow paste and vanilla. Pour batter into two greased 8-inch layer cake pans and bake at 375° for 30 to 35 minutes. Frost with a chocolate frosting.

❧ Devil's Food Cake

(TWO 8-INCH LAYER PANS)

⅔ cup shortening
⅔ cup sugar
1 teaspoon soda
1 teaspoon salt
1 teaspoon vanilla extract
⅔ cup unsulphured molasses

3 squares bitter chocolate or
   9 tablespoons cocoa
2 eggs
¾ cup sour milk
1½ cups sifted all-purpose flour

Cream together shortening, sugar, soda, salt, and vanilla. Stir in molasses. Melt chocolate over hot water; add to shortening-sugar mixture. Beat in eggs. Add sour milk alternately with flour (about ½ cup at each time). Put batter in two well-greased and lightly floured 8-inch layer cake pans. Bake at 375° for 25 minutes or until cake tests done. Cool and frost as desired. Yield: 10 to 12 servings.

❧ Devil's Food Layer Cake

(TWO 8-INCH LAYER PANS)

½ cup vegetable shortening
1¼ cups sugar
2 eggs
2 (1-ounce) squares
   unsweetened chocolate,
   melted

1¾ cups cake flour
½ teaspoon salt
1½ teaspoons soda
1 cup buttermilk
1 teaspoon vanilla extract

Thoroughly blend shortening and sugar. Add eggs and melted chocolate and beat until smooth. Combine flour, salt, and soda and add to creamed mixture alternately with buttermilk and vanilla mixture. Beat well. Put batter into two greased and floured 8-inch layer pans. Bake at 350° for 30 to 35 minutes. Frost.

❧ Red Devil's Food Cake No. 1

(TWO 8-INCH LAYER PANS)

1⅝ cups all-purpose flour (1½ cups
    plus 2 tablespoons)
1½ cups sugar
1¼ teaspoons soda
1 teaspoon salt
½ cup cocoa

½ cup shortening
1 cup milk
1 teaspoon vanilla extract
2 medium eggs, unbeaten (⅓
    to ½ cup)

Have all ingredients at room temperature. Sift together flour, sugar, soda, salt, and cocoa. Add shortening, milk, and vanilla, and beat with electric mixer at slow to medium speed for 2 minutes, scraping sides and bottom of bowl frequently. Add unbeaten eggs and beat 2 minutes longer, scraping bowl frequently. Pour batter into two greased and floured 8-inch layer cake pans. Bake at 350° for 30 to 35 minutes. When cake is cool, frost as desired.

❧ Red Devil's Food Cake No. 2

(TWO 8-INCH LAYER PANS)

1½ cups sifted cake flour
¾ teaspoon salt
¾ teaspoon soda
1¼ cups sugar
½ cup shortening (at room
    temperature)

⅔ cup water
2 squares unsweetened
    chocolate, melted
2 eggs
1 teaspoon vanilla extract

Combine flour, salt, soda, and sugar in sifter. Stir shortening just to soften. Sift in dry ingredients. Add water and mix until all flour is dampened. Then beat 2 minutes at low speed on electric mixer or 300 vigorous strokes by hand. Add melted chocolate, eggs, and vanilla and beat 1 minute longer in mixer or 150 strokes by hand. Batter will be very thin. Pour batter in two 8-inch layer pans which have been greased and lined with paper. Bake at 350° for 25 to 30 minutes. Cool and frost as desired.

❦ White Coconut Cake

(TWO 8-INCH LAYER PANS)

2½ cups sifted cake flour	1 teaspoon vanilla extract
3 teaspoons baking powder	2 teaspoons coconut flavoring
½ teaspoon salt	1 (3½-ounce) can flaked
½ cup soft shortening	coconut
1 cup sugar	4 egg whites
1 cup milk	⅓ cup sugar

Sift flour with baking powder and salt and set aside. Beat shortening until creamy. Gradually add 1 cup sugar, beating until very light and fluffy. At low speed, beat in flour mixture alternately with milk, beginning and ending with flour mixture; beat only until combined. Stir in vanilla, coconut flavoring, and coconut.

In medium bowl, beat egg whites until soft peaks form when beater is raised slowly. Gradually add ⅓ cup sugar, beating until stiff peaks form. Fold beaten egg whites into batter. Put batter into two greased, paper-lined, 8-inch layer cake pans. Bake at 350° about 25 to 30 minutes.

Let cool 10 minutes, then gently remove from pans. Cool completely on wire rack. Frost with Coconut Frosting.

❦ Heavenly Coconut Cake

(10-INCH TUBE PAN)

1 cup vegetable shortening	2 cups all-purpose flour
2 cups sugar	1 teaspoon salt
1 teaspoon vanilla extract	1 can flaked coconut
6 eggs	

Cream shortening and sugar; add vanilla and beat well. Add eggs, one at a time, beating well after each addition. Combine flour and salt and add to creamed mixture. Fold in coconut. Pour batter into a greased and floured 10-inch tube pan and bake at 325° for 1 hour and 20 minutes or until cake tests done.

❦ Coconut Mist Cake

(THREE 9-INCH LAYER PANS)

3 cups sifted cake flour
2 teaspoons baking powder
½ teaspoon salt
1 cup butter or shortening
1 pound (3½ cups) powdered
  sugar
4 egg yolks, well beaten
1 cup milk
1 teaspoon vanilla extract
1 cup shredded coconut
  (optional)
4 egg whites, stiffly beaten

Sift flour once, measure; add baking powder and salt, and sift together three times. Cream butter thoroughly, add sugar gradually, and cream together until light and fluffy. Add egg yolks and beat well. Add flour alternately with milk, a small amount at a time, beating until smooth after each addition. Add vanilla and coconut. Fold in egg whites quickly and thoroughly. Bake in three greased 9-inch layer pans at 375° for 25 to 30 minutes. Cool; frost with Never Fail Frosting and sprinkle with coconut.

❦ Coconut Cake

(THREE OR FOUR 9-INCH LAYER PANS)

1 cup butter
2 cups sugar
5 eggs
1 teaspoon soda
  Dash salt
2¾ cups cake flour
1 teaspoon baking powder
1 cup buttermilk
1 teaspoon vanilla extract
½ to ¾ teaspoon coconut
  flavoring
2 recipes Never Fail Frosting
2 cups fresh grated coconut

Cream butter and sugar until perfectly smooth (about 15 minutes on electric mixer). Add eggs, beating well after each addition. Sift dry ingredients together and add to creamed mixture alternately with buttermilk. Stir in vanilla and coconut flavoring. Bake in three or four greased and floured round 9-inch layer cake pans (number you use will depend on whether you like three thick layers or four thinner ones). Bake at 350° for about 25 minutes or until layers test done. Cool and frost. Sprinkle with coconut.

❧ Fresh Coconut Cake

(THREE 9-INCH LAYER PANS)

1 cup butter	1 cup milk
2 cups sugar	8 egg whites, beaten
3½ cups all-purpose flour	½ teaspoon vanilla extract
3½ teaspoons baking powder	½ teaspoon lemon extract

Cream the butter; add sugar gradually, continuing to cream well. Combine flour and baking powder and add to creamed mixture alternately with milk. Beat egg whites until stiff, but not dry. Fold into creamed mixture. Add extracts. Bake in three greased and floured 9-inch cake pans at 375° about 30 to 35 minutes or until browned. Cool before frosting.

❧ Coconut Chiffon Cake

(10-INCH TUBE PAN)

2 cups all-purpose flour	¾ cup cold water
1½ cups sugar	1 teaspoon vanilla extract
3 teaspoons baking powder	1 teaspoon almond extract
1 teaspoon salt	1 cup egg whites
½ cup salad oil	½ teaspoon cream of tartar
7 unbeaten egg yolks	¾ cup coconut

Sift dry ingredients into a bowl. Make a well and add oil, egg yolks, water, vanilla and almond extracts. Beat until smooth (1 minute on the mixer). Put egg whites and cream of tartar in a large bowl and beat until they form stiff peaks. Pour egg yolk mixture gradually over beaten whites, folding just until blended. Fold in coconut. Pour into ungreased 10-inch tube pan. Bake at 325° for 55 minutes, then increase to 350° for 10 to 15 minutes longer, until top springs back. Turn pan upside down until cake is cold before removing from pan. Remove from pan and frost with Fluffy Marshmallow Frosting.

℀ Orange-Coconut Cake

(TWO 8-INCH LAYER PANS)

½ cup butter
1⅓ cups sugar
2½ cups all-purpose flour
½ teaspoon salt
3 teaspoons baking powder

½ cup milk
½ cup orange juice
1½ teaspoons vanilla extract
3 egg whites

Cream butter and blend with sugar. Add dry ingredients alternately with milk and orange juice. Add vanilla, and fold in stiffly beaten egg whites. Bake in two greased 8-inch layer cake pans at 350° for 30 minutes. Put Orange Filling between layers.

℀ Lightly Lemon Coffeecake

(10-INCH TUBE PAN)

2 tablespoons vinegar
⅞ cup canned evaporated milk
1 teaspoon soda
½ cup soft butter or margarine
1 cup sugar
2 eggs, well beaten
1 teaspoon grated lemon rind
1¾ cups unsifted cake flour
2 teaspoons baking powder

½ teaspoon salt
½ cup brown sugar
1 tablespoon ground
   cinnamon
2 tablespoons lemon juice
1 cup sifted powdered sugar
Lemon peel, nuts, cherries
   (optional)

Combine vinegar and evaporated milk in small bowl; stir in soda. Cream butter and sugar together until fluffy; add eggs and lemon rind, and beat well. Sift flour, baking powder, and salt together; add alternately with milk mixture to creamed mixture, beating well. Mix brown sugar and cinnamon. Spread half of batter in greased, floured 10-inch tube pan; sprinkle with half the cinnamon-sugar. Add remaining batter; sprinkle with rest of cinnamon-sugar. Bake at 350° for about 45 to 50 minutes. Cool in pan 5 minutes; remove from pan. Mix lemon juice and powdered sugar, spoon over cake. Garnish with peel, nuts, or cherries. Serve warm. Yield: 16 servings.

❧ Honey-Crisp Coffeecake

(8- OR 9-INCH CAKE PAN)

1½ cups all-purpose flour	½ cup milk
2 teaspoons baking powder	3 tablespoons melted
½ teaspoon salt	shortening
½ cup sugar	Honey-Crisp Topping
1 egg, beaten	

Sift together flour, baking powder, salt, and sugar. Combine egg, milk, and melted shortening; add to flour mixture, stirring until mixture is smooth. Pour into greased 8- or 9-inch cake pan. Top with Honey-Crisp Topping and bake at 400° about 25 minutes.

Honey-Crisp Topping

3 tablespoons softened butter or margarine	½ cup crushed corn flakes
⅓ cup honey	½ cup drained crushed pineapple
¼ cup flaked coconut	

Cream together butter or margarine and honey until light and fluffy. Add remaining ingredients; mix thoroughly. Spread on coffeecake before baking.

❧ Quick Coffeecake

(TWO 9-INCH SQUARE PANS)

1 package white cake mix	1 tablespoon dry instant coffee
6 tablespoons butter, melted	½ cup chopped nuts (optional)
½ cup sugar	
½ teaspoon ground cinnamon	

Prepare cake mix according to directions on package. Pour batter into two greased 9- x 9- x 2-inch pans, and bake at 350° for 30 to 35 minutes.

Dribble melted butter over warm cake. Combine sugar, instant coffee, and cinnamon and sprinkle over cake. Chopped nuts may be added if desired. Yield: about 12 servings.

❦ Prune and Apricot Coffeecake

(9-INCH TUBE PAN)

¾ cup dried prunes	1 teaspoon vanilla extract
¾ cup dried apricots	⅔ cup brown sugar
¾ cup shortening	1 tablespoon all-purpose flour
¾ cup sugar	1 tablespoon ground
2 eggs	cinnamon
2 cups all-purpose flour	6 tablespoons melted butter or
2 teaspoons baking powder	margarine
½ teaspoon salt	⅓ cup chopped walnuts
¾ cup milk	

Soak fruit in hot water for 5 minutes. Drain and chop fine. Cream shortening and sugar; add eggs, one at a time, beating well after each addition. Sift together dry ingredients; add alternately with milk and vanilla to creamed mixture. Fold in chopped fruit.

Combine brown sugar, flour, and cinnamon. Pour one-third of fruit mixture into oiled and floured 9-inch tube pan. Sprinkle with one-third of brown sugar mixture and one-third of melted butter. Repeat twice. Sprinkle with nuts. Bake at 350° for 55 minutes. Cool in pan 25 minutes. Yield: 8 servings.

❦ Daisy Coffeecake

(BAKING SHEET)

2 packages dry yeast	2 eggs
¼ cup very warm water	2 tablespoons melted butter or
1 cup milk	margarine
½ cup sugar	¼ cup sugar
¼ cup shortening or oil	½ teaspoon ground cinnamon
2 teaspoons salt	Powdered sugar icing
About 5 cups all-purpose	(optional)
flour	

Soften yeast in water. Scald milk. Combine ½ cup sugar, shortening or oil, and salt in large bowl. Add hot milk, stirring until sugar dissolves and shortening is melted. Cool to lukewarm. Stir in about 1½ cups flour and beat well. Beat in softened yeast and eggs. Stir in enough additional flour to make a soft dough. Turn out on lightly floured board or pastry cloth and knead until smooth and satiny, 5 to 8 minutes.

Shape into ball and place in lightly greased bowl, turning to grease surface of ball. Cover and let rise in warm place (80° to 85°) until doubled, about 1½ hours. Punch down. Divide dough in half. Wait 10 minutes; then roll each half of dough to a 12-inch square about ¼ inch thick. Brush half of square with melted butter or margarine. Combine ¼ cup sugar and cinnamon. Sprinkle 4 teaspoons of this mixture over buttered half of dough. Fold unbuttered half over buttered half, sealing edges. Brush half of dough with butter or margarine and sprinkle with 2 teaspoons cinnamon-sugar. Fold in half again, sealing edges. Roll out to 12-inch circle. Place on greased baking sheet.

With scissors or sharp knife cut into 16 wedges, cutting to 1 inch of center. Twist each wedge three times in same direction.

Let rise in warm place until doubled, about 45 minutes.

Bake at 350° for 20 to 25 minutes or until golden brown. Brush with powdered sugar icing, if desired. Make icing by adding soft butter and a little cream to powdered sugar to make a thin mixture. Yield: 2 coffeecakes.

Jewish Coffeecake
(9-INCH LAYER PAN)

1 cup commercial sour cream	2 eggs
½ to ¾ teaspoon soda	1 teaspoon vanilla extract
1 cup margarine	1½ cups all-purpose flour
1 cup sugar	1½ teaspoons baking powder

Filling and Topping

½ cup brown sugar	1 teaspoon ground cinnamon
½ cup chopped pecans	

Mix together the cream and soda and let set for 1 hour. Cream together margarine and sugar; add eggs and vanilla and beat well. Add sour cream mixture. Stir in flour and baking powder, sifted together. Beat well. Combine brown sugar, pecans, and cinnamon.

Put half the batter mixture into a greased 9-inch layer pan. Spread half the topping on batter. Add rest of batter, then rest of topping. Bake at 350° for 40 minutes.

❧ Apple Coffeecake

(13- x 9- x 2-INCH PAN)

½ cup shortening
1 cup sugar
1 teaspoon vanilla extract
1 teaspoon salt
2 eggs
2½ cups all-purpose flour
1 teaspoon baking powder

1 teaspoon soda
1 cup commercial sour cream
2 cups peeled, chopped apples
½ cup chopped black walnuts
½ cup brown sugar
1 teaspoon ground cinnamon

Cream together shortening, sugar, vanilla, and salt. Add eggs and beat well. Sift together flour, baking powder, and soda; add to creamed mixture alternately with sour cream. Fold in chopped apples.

Pour batter into a greased 13- x 9- x 2-inch pan. Sprinkle top evenly with chopped black walnuts. Combine brown sugar and cinnamon and sprinkle over nuts. Bake at 350° for 25 to 30 minutes. Yield: 12 servings.

❧ Apple-Cheese Coffeecake

(9-INCH SQUARE PAN)

1½ cups all-purpose flour
2 teaspoons baking powder
¾ teaspoon salt
¼ cup shortening
½ cup sugar
1 egg

¾ cup milk
1 cup shredded sharp cheese
1 cup sliced apples
¼ cup brown sugar
½ teaspoon ground cinnamon
1 tablespoon melted butter

Sift together flour, baking powder, and salt. Cream together shortening and sugar until light and fluffy. Add egg and beat well. Add dry ingredients alternately with milk, mixing well. Blend in cheese and pour into 9- x 9- x 2-inch greased pan. Arrange apple slices on top. Combine brown sugar, cinnamon, and butter, and sprinkle over top of apples. Bake at 375° about 35 minutes.

❦ Sour Cream Coffeecake No. 1

(BUNDT PAN)

1 cup butter or margarine	1 teaspoon baking powder
2 cups sugar	¼ teaspoon salt
2 eggs	1 cup chopped pecans
1 cup commercial sour cream	4 tablespoons brown sugar
1 teaspoon vanilla extract	1 teaspoon ground cinnamon
2 cups all-purpose flour	

Cream butter and sugar well. Add eggs, one at a time, beating well after each addition. Fold in sour cream and vanilla. Add dry ingredients which have been sifted together. Pour half of this batter into greased and floured Bundt pan or an angel food cake pan.

Mix together pecans, brown sugar, and cinnamon. Sprinkle three-fourths of the mixture on batter; do not let nut mixture touch side of pan. Top with rest of batter and sprinkle rest of nut mixture on top. Bake at 350° for 45 to 60 minutes. Cool cake for 10 minutes before turning out of pan.

❦ Sour Cream Coffecake No. 2

(10-INCH TUBE PAN)

2 sticks butter or margarine	¼ teaspoon salt
1½ cups sugar	½ teaspoon soda
1 cup commercial sour cream	1 cup finely chopped nuts
2 eggs, well beaten	1½ teaspoons sugar
1 teaspoon vanilla extract	2½ teaspoons ground
2 cups all-purpose flour	cinnamon
1 teaspoon baking powder	

Cream butter, sugar, and sour cream; add eggs and vanilla and beat well. Combine dry ingredients and add to creamed mixture; beat well. Thoroughly grease a 10-inch tube pan.

Make topping by combining chopped nuts, sugar, and cinnamon. In bottom of the well-greased tube pan put a third of topping mixture; alternate layers of batter and topping, ending with batter. Bake at 350° for 45 minutes.

❧ Cranberry Sauce Cake

(9-INCH TUBE PAN)

1½ cups whole cranberry sauce	⅓ cup orange juice
1 cup walnuts or pecans	Grated rind of 1 orange
3 cups all-purpose flour	1 teaspoon soda
1½ cups sugar	1 teaspoon salt
1 cup mayonnaise	

Lightly grease a 9-inch tube pan and line bottom with brown paper. Combine cranberry sauce, nuts, mayonnaise, orange juice, and rind. Sift flour, sugar, soda, and salt on top. Stir until mixture is well blended. Pour into tube pan. Bake at 350° about 1 hour and 15 minutes, or until cake tests done. Cool.

Topping

2 tablespoons margarine	¼ cup whole cranberry sauce
2 cups sifted powdered sugar	

Cream margarine. Add sugar and cranberry sauce; beat until creamy. Frost cooled cake.

❧ Cranberry-Nut Cake

(TWO 9-INCH LAYER PANS)

2½ cups all-purpose flour	⅛ teaspoon red food coloring
1 teaspoon baking powder	1 teaspoon vanilla extract
1 teaspoon salt	3 eggs, beaten
1 teaspoon ground nutmeg	¾ cup milk
½ teaspoon soda	¾ cup whole cranberry sauce
1 cup shortening	½ cup chopped nuts
1 cup sugar	

Sift together flour, baking powder, salt, nutmeg, and soda. Cream together shortening and sugar, and add food coloring and vanilla extract. Add beaten eggs; mix well. Add flour mixture alternately with milk and whole cranberry sauce, beating well after each addition. Fold in nuts. Bake in two greased and floured, waxed paper-lined 9-inch round pans at 350° about 35 minutes. Put Seven-Minute Frosting between layers and over sides and top of cake.

Note: Do not combine milk and cranberry sauce; add milk after first addition of flour, and cranberry sauce after second addition.

❧ Cupcakes

(CUPCAKE PANS)

1 cup butter	1 teaspoon ground nutmeg
2 cups sugar	½ teaspoon soda
4 eggs	1 cup milk
All-purpose flour, enough to make mixture as thick as pound cake (about 4 cups)	

Cream butter and sugar until well blended. Add eggs, one at a time, and beat well. Sift flour and add nutmeg and soda. Add to mixture alternately with milk. Bake in cupcake pans at 350° for 35 to 40 minutes. Yield: about 3 dozen 2-inch cupcakes.

❧ Orange Cupcakes

(BAKING CUPS)

½ cup shortening or butter	2 cups all-purpose flour
1 cup sugar	½ teaspoon salt
2 eggs	1 cup raisins or dates
1 teaspoon soda	1 cup chopped pecans
⅔ cup buttermilk	Orange Syrup

Cream shortening or butter with sugar. Add eggs and beat. Add soda to buttermilk and stir well. Add dry ingredients to creamed mixture alternately with buttermilk Add fruit and nuts. Put in small baking cups and bake at 375° for about 12 minutes. Pour Orange Syrup over each cupcake.

Orange Syrup

1 cup sugar	1 tablespoon grated orange rind
1 cup orange juice	

Add sugar to orange juice and grated orange rind. Bring to a boil and pour a tablespoon (or less) over each cooked cupcake.

❧ Different Cupcakes

(MUFFIN PANS)

4 squares unsweetened chocolate	1¾ cups sugar
2 sticks margarine	1 cup all-purpose flour
¼ teaspoon butter flavoring	4 large eggs
1½ cups broken pecan meats	1 teaspoon vanilla extract

Melt chocolate and margarine in a heavy pan. Add butter flavoring and pecans and stir to coat pecans. Remove from heat.

Combine sugar, flour, eggs, and vanilla and mix only until blended. Do not beat. Add chocolate-nut mixture and again mix carefully, but do not beat. Put into 18 baking cups set in muffin pans. Bake at 325° about 30 to 35 minutes.

❧ Date Delight Cake

(TWO 8-INCH LAYER PANS)

½ cup vegetable shortening	2 eggs
1 cup sugar	2 cups sifted cake flour
½ teaspoon salt	2½ teaspoons baking powder
1 teaspoon lemon extract	¾ cup milk

Blend shortening, sugar, salt, flavoring, and eggs. Sift flour with baking powder. Add to shortening alternately with milk. Pour into two greased 8-inch pans and bake at 350° for 30 minutes. Spread with Date Delight Filling and frost as desired.

❧ Texas Date Cake

(9-INCH TUBE PAN)

1 cup chopped dates	1 egg
1 teaspoon soda	1 teaspoon vanilla extract
1 cup boiling water	1⅓ cups all-purpose flour
½ cup butter or margarine	1 cup pecans
2 cups sugar	

Put chopped dates and soda in large bowl; add boiling water. Mash until as smooth as mush. (This is a most important step. It takes time, but is worth it). Cream butter or margarine and 1 cup of the sugar. Add the other cup of sugar, the egg, and vanilla. Stir in the date mixture. Then add flour and pecans. Bake in a greased tube pan at 350° for about 1 hour.

❦ Date-Nut Loaf
(LOAF PAN)

½ cup butter or margarine
1 cup brown sugar
2 egg yolks, beaten
2 cups all-purpose flour
½ teaspoon salt
1 pound dates, chopped

1 cup chopped nuts
1 teaspoon soda
½ cup lukewarm water
1 teaspoon vanilla extract
2 egg whites

Cream butter and margarine. Add beaten egg yolks. Combine flour and salt and put half the mixture over chopped dates and nuts. Stir to coat. Dissolve soda in water. Add flour to creamed mixture alternately with water. Stir in vanilla and then stir in dates and nuts. Fold in egg whites. Put batter in greased loaf pan. Bake at 275° for 1¼ to 1½ hours, or until cake tests done.

❦ Date-Nut-Mayonnaise Cake
(TWO 8-INCH LAYER PANS OR LOAF PAN)

1 cup sugar
½ teaspoon salt
3 tablespoons cocoa
1 teaspoon ground cinnamon
1 cup mayonnaise

1 cup dates or raisins
1 cup chopped walnuts
1 teaspoon soda
1 cup boiling water
2 cups all-purpose flour

Mix sugar, salt, cocoa, and cinnamon. Add mayonnaise and blend. Mix dates and nuts and pour hot water and soda over them. Add to mayonnaise mix. Add flour and blend in thoroughly. Bake at 350° for 40 to 45 minutes in greased loaf pan or 35 to 40 minutes in two 8- or 9-inch greased layer pans. Serve with whipped cream frosting or cut in squares to serve.

❧ Date-Nut Loaf Cake

(10-INCH TUBE PAN)

1 cup butter
2 cups sugar
4 eggs
3 cups all-purpose flour
¼ teaspoon salt
1 teaspoon soda
2 tablespoons orange juice

½ cup buttermilk
1 cup chopped dates
1 cup chopped nuts
1 cup grated or flaked
    coconut
Orange Sauce

Cream butter and sugar together until light and fluffy. Add eggs, one at a time, beating well after each addition. Sift together flour and salt and set aside. Add soda and orange juice to buttermilk.

Add dry ingredients to creamed mixture alternately with buttermilk, beginning and ending with flour mixture. Stir in dates, nuts, and coconut. Spoon mixture into greased 10-inch tube pan and bake at 350° from 1 to 1¼ hours or until cake tests done. Remove from pan and drizzle with Orange Sauce while cake is still hot.

Orange Sauce

2 tablespoons grated orange rind   1 cup orange juice
2 cups powdered sugar

Mix well together and spoon over Date-Nut Loaf Cake while it is still hot.

❧ Date-Chocolate Cake

(TUBE PAN)

½ cup shortening
1¼ cups brown sugar
2 eggs
2 (1-ounce) squares
    unsweetened chocolate
1½ cups all-purpose flour
1 teaspoon soda
½ teaspoon salt

1 cup milk
1 cup chopped dates
½ cup diced marshmallows
¼ cup all-purpose flour
1 teaspoon vanilla extract
1 cup chopped pecans, if
    desired

Cream shortening; add sugar, creaming well. Add eggs, one at a time, beating well. Melt chocolate over hot water; add. Sift together

54

1½ cups flour, soda, and salt; add alternately with milk. Mix dates, marshmallows, and ¼ cup flour. Add to batter with vanilla. Add pecans, if desired. Pour into greased tube pan. Bake at 350° for about 1 hour. Cool on wire rack.

❧ Four-Egg Cake

(THREE 8-INCH LAYER PANS)

¾ cup shortening	4 teaspoons baking powder
1¾ cups sugar	¾ teaspoon salt
4 egg yolks, beaten	1 cup milk
3 cups cake or 2½ cups all-purpose flour	1 teaspoon vanilla extract
	4 egg whites, beaten

Cream shortening for about 2 minutes. Add sugar gradually, continue creaming about 1½ minutes after all sugar is added. Add yolks beaten very light. Beat about 2 minutes. Add sifted dry ingredients alternately with the milk and vanilla. Begin and end with flour mixture. Fold in stiffly beaten whites. Pour into three greased 8-inch pans and bake at 350° for about 50 minutes. Frost as desired.

❧ Four-Egg Rich Cake

(TWO 8- OR 9-INCH LAYER PANS)

1 cup butter	¼ teaspoon salt
1½ cups sugar	1 cup light cream
4 egg yolks	1 teaspoon vanilla extract
2 cups all-purpose flour	4 egg whites, beaten
3 teaspoons baking powder	

Cream butter and sugar and add 1 unbeaten egg yolk at a time. Mix well. Combine flour, baking powder, and salt, and add alternately with the cream and vanilla. Fold in stiffly beaten egg whites. Bake in two greased 8- or 9-inch layers at 350° for 25 to 30 minutes. Frost with Coconut or Chocolate Fudge Frosting.

❦ Two-Egg Cake
(TWO 8-INCH LAYER PANS)

½ cup shortening
1 cup plus 2 tablespoons sugar
2 eggs, unbeaten
1¾ cups sifted cake flour

2¼ teaspoons baking powder
½ teaspoon salt
¾ cup milk
1 teaspoon vanilla extract

Cream shortening until smooth. Gradually add sugar, and beat until light and fluffy. Add eggs, one at a time, beating well after each addition. Sift flour, baking powder, and salt together. Add to creamed mixture alternately with milk, beginning and ending with flour mixture. Stir in vanilla. Put batter in two greased 8-inch layer pans lined with paper. Bake at 375° for 25 to 30 minutes. Frost as desired.

❦ Peggy's Magic Fruitcake
(LOAF PAN)

1 (15½-ounce) can sweetened
    condensed milk
1 cup chopped nuts

3 cups flaked coconut
1 pound pitted dates, chopped

Thoroughly blend sweetened condensed milk, nuts, coconut, and chopped dates. Pack in buttered loaf pan and bake at 375° for 25 minutes, or until brown. Remove from pan and let cool thoroughly. Cut in thin slices.

❦ Fruitcake
(2- OR 3-POUND PANS)

3 pounds white raisins
1 pint fresh orange juice
2 pounds dates
3 or 4 quarts all-purpose flour
1¾ pounds butter
2 pounds sugar
24 eggs
2 tablespoons vanilla extract

1 tablespoon salt
2 pounds candied cherries
    (use red and green fruit)
2 pounds candied pineapple
1½ pounds citron
1 pound shelled almonds
3 quarts or more shelled
    pecans

Soak raisins overnight in orange juice. Next morning, dredge the soaked raisins and the dates (which have been cut into small pieces) in flour, using as much as can be taken up. In a large pan, cream butter and sugar thoroughly. Beat eggs separately. Add yolks first, then vanilla and salt. Add raisins, dates, cherries (whole), pineapple (cut in not-too-small pieces), citron, and the last of all, nuts. Leave pecans in halves and almonds whole. Now add stiffly beaten egg whites. Line bottoms of pans with well-greased brown paper. For best results, bake in 2- or 3-pound pans at 250° for 1½ hours; then reduce heat to 225° for 1 hour. This will make 18 to 20 pounds of fruitcake. Wrap in cellophane while still hot and store until needed.

❦ Kentucky Bourbon Fruitcake

(ONE LARGE MOLD)

¾ pound butter	1 cup chopped candied
2 cups sugar	pineapple
6 eggs	1 cup chopped candied
½ cup molasses	cherries
4 cups all-purpose flour	1 cup orange marmalade
1 heaping teaspoon baking	2 pounds shelled pecans,
powder	chopped
2 teaspoons ground nutmeg	1 large cup bourbon
1 pound raisins	Apple slices

Cream butter and sugar; add eggs, one at a time, beating well after each addition. Add molasses and mix well. Sift together flour, baking powder, and ground nutmeg. Put fruits, marmalade, and nuts in large bowl. Add about 1 cup of flour mixture and stir to coat fruit. Add remainder of flour to creamed mixture alternately with whiskey. Stir in fruits and nuts.

Grease one large mold or two smaller ones (two large loaf pans are right size); line with heavy brown paper which has been greased. Spoon batter into pans and cover with greased brown paper. Bake at 250° until toothpick or cake tester inserted in center comes out clean (about 2½ to 3 hours).

Wrap cake in cloth which has been dampened with whiskey; place in a tin container. Add apple slices and cover container. Let sit until cake has "ripened." A month would not be too long to let ripen.

❦ Famous Old Fruitcake

(LOAF PANS)

1 pound candied grapefruit
    peel or citron
1 pound candied pineapple
1 pound candied red
    watermelon rind or
    cherries
3 pounds seeded raisins or
    currants
1½ pounds figs, dates, or
    apricots
4 cups all-purpose flour
1 teaspoon ground cinnamon
½ teaspoon ground cloves

1 teaspoon ground nutmeg
¼ teaspoon ground allspice
½ teaspoon salt
½ pound butter or margarine
1 cup brown sugar, well
    packed
6 eggs, separated
½ cup fruit juice or sweet
    pickle syrup
½ pound almonds
1 pound pecans or black
    walnuts

Cut grapefruit peel, candied pineapple, and watermelon rind in ½-inch cubes. Leave cherries, raisins, and nuts whole. Sift flour, spices, and salt. Cream butter or margarine and sugar in another bowl. Add beaten egg yolks to creamed mixture. Mix a small amount of the flour mixture with raisins and dates to keep them from sticking together. Add flour mixtures alternately with fruit juice to the creamed mixture. Add fruits and nuts. Mix thoroughly. Add beaten egg whites.

Grease pans. Line with brown paper, and extend 1 inch above pans. Grease paper. Pack batter firmly into pans with hands to ½ inch of top of pan. Cover top with waxed paper and place pan of water in oven under cakes. Bake at 250° for the following lengths of time: for 1-pound cake, 2 to 2½ hours; a 2-pound cake, 3½ hours; a 3-pound cake, 4 hours. Remove waxed paper from top of cake during last 15 minutes of baking. Yield: 11 pounds.

❦ Lemon-Pecan Fruitcake

(TWO LOAF PANS)

1 box brown sugar
1 pound margarine
6 egg yolks, beaten
2 cups all-purpose flour
1 teaspoon baking powder
2 ounces lemon extract
1 quart chopped pecans

½ pound candied pineapple,
    chopped
½ pound candied cherries,
    chopped
2 cups all-purpose flour
6 egg whites, beaten

Cream together sugar and margarine until smooth; add beaten egg yolks and mix well. Combine 2 cups flour and baking powder and add to the creamed mixture. Add lemon extract. Coat pecans, pineapple, and cherries with 2 cups flour and add to creamed mixture. Fold in beaten egg whites. Cover and let stand overnight.

The next day, put mixture into two greased loaf pans and bake at 250° for 1½ hours.

❧ Japanese Fruitcake
(THREE 8-INCH LAYER PANS)

1 cup butter or margarine	1 teaspoon ground cloves
2½ cups sugar	1 teaspoon ground allspice
½ cup milk	1 teaspoon ground cinnamon
6 eggs, beaten	2 teaspoons baking powder
4 cups all-purpose flour	1 cup chopped nuts
¼ teaspoon salt	1 cup seedless raisins

Cream butter or margarine and sugar; add milk. Beat well. Add beaten eggs. Sift together dry ingredients; mix into batter, and add nuts and raisins. Reserve 1¾ cups of batter to put in frosting. Bake in three greased 8-inch cake pans at 375° about 25 minutes. Frost with Japanese Fruitcake Frosting.

❧ Refrigerator Fruitcake
(ASSORTED MOLDS)

¾ pound butter or margarine	2 teaspoons vanilla extract
1 pound marshmallows	½ pound candied cherries, chopped
1 pound graham cracker crumbs	¼ pound candied citron, cut fine
1 pound shelled pecans	½ pound candied pineapple, chopped
4 tablespoons brown sugar	
2 (8-ounce) boxes pitted dates	

In the top of a double boiler, melt the butter or margarine and the marshmallows. In a large bowl, put other ingredients; add melted mixture and mix well. Mold or shape into rolls or loaves. Wrap in waxed paper and store in refrigerator. Cut or slice to serve.

❦ Dried Apple Fruitcake
(10-INCH TUBE PAN)

2 cups dried apples
1 cup molasses
1 cup butter or margarine
1 cup sugar
2 eggs
4 cups all-purpose flour
2 teaspoons soda
1 teaspoon ground cinnamon

¾ teaspoon ground allspice
¾ teaspoon ground cloves
½ teaspoon ground nutmeg
1 cup buttermilk
2 pounds seedless raisins
½ cup chopped citron
1 teaspoon vanilla extract

Soak apples in water overnight, and cook in molasses until thick. Cream butter or margarine and sugar; add eggs. Sift flour with soda and spices; add to butter mixture alternately with buttermilk. Add raisins and citron, vanilla, and apples. Bake in a 10-inch tube pan, greased and lined with oiled paper, at 250° about 2 to 2½ hours.

❦ Butterscotch-Fruitcake Miniatures
(40 SMALL CUPCAKES)

½ cup butter or margarine
½ cup sugar
3 eggs
1¼ cups all-purpose flour
1 teaspoon ground cinnamon
½ teaspoon baking powder
½ teaspoon salt
½ teaspoon ground nutmeg

¼ teaspoon ground cloves
1 teaspoon vanilla extract
1 cup chopped walnuts
1 cup mixed candied fruit,
  finely chopped
½ cup raisins
1 (6-ounce) package
  butterscotch pieces

Cream butter; gradually add sugar, creaming thoroughly. Add eggs one at a time, beating well after each addition. Combine 1 cup flour, cinnamon, baking powder, salt, nutmeg, and cloves. Gradually stir into creamed mixture. Add vanilla. Toss together walnuts, candied fruit, raisins, butterscotch pieces, and remaining ¼ cup flour; stir into batter. Place paper baking cups in 1¾-inch cupcake or muffin pans. Spoon in fruitcake mixture. Bake at 300° about 40 minutes.

❦ Dundee Cakes

(1-POUND TIN CANS)

¾ pound butter
1 pound brown sugar
8 eggs
1 pound seedless raisins,
  chopped
1 pound currants, chopped
½ cup chopped candied
  cherries

1 pound candied peel
  (grapefruit, orange, and
  lemon), chopped
2 cups chopped nuts
8 cups all-purpose flour
1 cup fruit juice (grape or
  citrus)

Cream the butter and sugar until light and fluffy; add eggs, one at a time, beating well after each addition. Chop the fruit, candied peel, and nuts. Dredge the chopped fruits with a little of the flour. Add the sifted flour to the creamed butter and sugar. Add fruit juice and beat well. Stir in the fruit and nuts and when well mixed, pour into 1-pound tins, which have been greased and lined with brown paper. Bake at 350° 50 to 60 minutes. Yield: about 10 pounds.

❦ Light Fruitcake

(TWO 9-INCH SPRINGFORM PANS)

2 cups all-purpose flour
2 teaspoons baking powder
½ teaspoon salt
1 pound coarsely chopped
  candied pineapple
1 pound candied cherries, left
  whole

1½ pounds coarsely chopped
  pitted dates
4 eggs
1 cup sugar
2 pounds pecan halves (8
  cups)

Combine flour, baking powder, and salt. Add fruits and mix well to coat with flour. Beat eggs until light and fluffy. Gradually beat in sugar. Add fruit-flour mixture and nuts; mix well with hands. Grease pans (two 9-inch springform pans or angel food pan and assorted molds as desired). Line pans with greased brown paper. Divide mixture between pans and press firmly into pans. Bake at 275° about 1¼ hours or until cakes test done. Let cakes stand in pans about 10 minutes; turn out on racks and remove brown paper. Cool well before wrapping for storage. Yield: about 6 pounds.

❧ White Fruitcake No. 1

(LOAF PANS)

1 cup shortening	½ pound candied citron
2 cups sugar	½ pound candied pineapple
4 cups all-purpose flour, divided	½ pound candied orange peel
2 teaspoons baking powder	½ pound candied lemon peel
½ teaspoon salt	½ pound candied cherries
1 cup water	1 pound blanched almonds
1 pound seeded white raisins	8 egg whites, beaten

Cream shortening and add sugar gradually. Add one-half the sifted flour, the baking powder, and salt to the creamed mixture. Add water and mix well. Chop fruit and nuts and add remaining flour and mix well. Stir into creamed mixture, and fold in well-beaten egg whites. Bake in well-greased loaf pans at 250° to 300° for 3 hours. Yield: 10 pounds.

❧ White Fruitcake No. 2

(TWO TUBE PANS)

1 pound candied cherries	4 cups all-purpose flour
1 pound candied pineapple	2 teaspoons baking powder
½ pound citron	1 teaspoon soda
2 pounds white raisins	1 pound butter
1 pound chopped nuts	2 cups sugar
2 (8-ounce) packages coconut	10 eggs

Cut fruit in small pieces and mix with nuts and coconut. Combine flour, baking powder, and soda and add to fruit. Cream butter and sugar until light and fluffy. Add eggs, one at a time, beating after each addition. Add first mixture and mix well. Bake in two greased tube pans at 250° for 3 hours. Yield: about 10 pounds.

❦ Whole Wheat Gingerbread
(9- x 9- x 2-inch pan)

¼ cup butter
½ cup sugar
1 egg, well beaten
½ cup molasses
½ cup sour milk
1¾ cups whole wheat flour

½ teaspoon soda
2 teaspoons baking powder
1½ teaspoons cinnamon or
    allspice
1 teaspoon ground ginger
¼ teaspoon salt

Cream butter and sugar until smooth. Add well-beaten egg. Mix molasses and milk together. Mix flour with soda, baking powder, spices, and salt. Add dry ingredients to creamed mixture alternately with liquid, adding flour first and last. Bake in a greased 9-inch square pan at 350° for 35 to 40 minutes.

❦ Sour Milk Gingerbread
(13- x 9- x 2-inch pan)

¾ cup shortening
1 cup brown sugar
1 cup molasses
3 eggs, beaten
3 cups all-purpose flour
1 teaspoon soda
1 teaspoon baking powder

½ teaspoon salt
2 tablespoons ground ginger
½ teaspoon ground cloves
1 tablespoon ground
    cinnamon
1 cup sour milk

Cream shortening. Gradually add sugar, beating well after each addition. Add molasses and beaten eggs. Mix. Sift dry ingredients together. Add dry ingredients alternately with milk to molasses mixture. Pour into well-greased 13- x 9- x 2-inch pan lined with waxed paper. Bake at 325° for 25 minutes.

🦌 Gingerbread

(13- x 9- x 2-INCH PAN)

2 eggs, beaten	2 teaspoons ground ginger
¾ cup brown sugar	1½ teaspoons ground cinnamon
¾ cup molasses	½ teaspoon ground cloves
¾ cup cooking oil	½ teaspoon ground nutmeg
2½ cups all-purpose flour	½ teaspoon baking powder
2 teaspoons soda	1 cup boiling water

Add beaten eggs to brown sugar, molasses, and oil. Combine dry ingredients and sift; add to egg mixture. Stir in boiling water. Bake in a greased 13- x 9- x 2-inch pan at 350° for 25 minutes or until cake is springy to the touch. Yield: 16 servings.

🦌 Hot Water Gingerbread No. 1

(LOAF PAN).

⅓ cup shortening	2 teaspoons soda
⅔ cup boiling water	1 teaspoon salt
1 cup sorghum molasses	1 teaspoon ground cinnamon
1 egg	1½ teaspoons ground ginger
2¾ cups all-purpose flour	¼ teaspoon ground cloves

Melt shortening in boiling water; add sorghum and well-beaten egg, then the dry ingredients sifted together. Bake in greased loaf pan at 350° about 30 minutes.

🦌 Hot Water Gingerbread No. 2

(11- x 8-INCH PAN)

2 cups sifted cake flour	½ teaspoon salt
2 teaspoons soda	½ cup shortening
1 teaspoon ground nutmeg	1 cup brown sugar
2 teaspoons ground ginger	2 eggs
½ teaspoon ground cloves	½ cup boiling water
½ teaspoon ground cinnamon	½ cup molasses

Sift all dry ingredients together three times. Cream shortening; add sugar and unbeaten eggs; beat all thoroughly. Add to dry ingredients, mixing thoroughly; add boiling water and molasses mixed together. (Will be a rather thin batter.) Bake in greased paper-lined 11- x 8-inch pan at 350° about 30 minutes, or until done. Allow to remain in pan 5 minutes after removing from oven; then cool on wire rack.

🍂 Old-Fashioned Gingerbread

(13- x 9- x 2-INCH PAN)

⅓ cup shortening	2 cups all-purpose flour
1 cup sugar	1 teaspoon soda
2 eggs	½ teaspoon salt
½ cup molasses	1½ teaspoons ground ginger
1 cup commercial sour cream	¼ teaspoon ground cloves

Cream shortening and sugar; add eggs, one at a time, beating well after each addition. Stir in molasses and sour cream. Blend sifted dry ingredients into creamed mixture; beat 2 minutes at medium speed. Bake in greased 13- x 9- x 2-inch pan at 350° for 35 minutes, or until cake tests done.

🍂 Sour Cream Gingerbread

(11¼- x 7¼- x 2-INCH PAN)

1 cup light brown sugar	½ teaspoon ground nutmeg
2 cups all-purpose flour	2 eggs
¾ teaspoon soda	2 tablespoons vegetable oil
1½ teaspoons ground ginger	1 cup commercial sour cream
1 teaspoon salt	½ cup unsulphured molasses

Sift together the first six ingredients and set aside. Beat eggs, oil, sour cream, and molasses just until well blended. Add dry ingredients and stir to mix well. Spoon into a greased 11¼- x 7¼- x 2-inch pan. Bake at 350° about 30 minutes. Yield: 10 to 12 servings.

❦ Gold Cake

(TWO 8-INCH LAYER PANS)

2 cups sifted cake flour	¾ cup milk
1⅓ cups sugar	4 egg yolks
1 teaspoon salt	½ cup milk
3 teaspoons baking powder	1 teaspoon lemon extract
½ cup vegetable shortening	

Combine flour, sugar, salt, and baking powder in mixing bowl. Add shortening and the ¾ cup milk. Beat vigorously with mixer for 2 minutes. Add egg yolks, ½ cup milk, and lemon flavoring. Pour batter into two greased, floured, and paper-lined 8-inch layer cake pans. Bake at 350° for 30 to 35 minutes.

❦ Gold Loaf Cake

(LOAF PAN)

½ cup butter or margarine	½ cup milk
1 cup sugar	½ teaspoon lemon or vanilla
1½ cups all-purpose flour	extract
1 teaspoon baking powder	4 egg yolks, beaten

Cream the butter and sugar. Mix dry ingredients and add to creamed mixture alternately with the milk. Add vanilla or lemon extract. Fold in beaten egg yolks. Bake in a greased loaf pan at 350° about 40 minutes.

❦ Prize Gold Cake

(9-INCH TUBE PAN)

8 egg yolks	3 cups all-purpose flour
2 cups white sugar	2 teaspoons baking powder
1 cup butter or margarine	½ teaspoon salt
1 cup milk	1 teaspoon lemon extract

Beat egg yolks well; add sugar and beat to a cream. Add butter, milk, flour, baking powder, and salt together. Add flavoring. Bake in greased 9-inch tube pan at 300° for 1¼ hours.

❧ Autumn Gold Cake

(TWO 8-INCH LAYER PANS)

2¼ cups sifted cake flour
¼ teaspoon soda
3 teaspoons baking powder
½ teaspoon salt
1½ teaspoons pumpkin pie spice
½ cup shortening
¾ cup brown sugar

¾ cup granulated sugar
2 eggs
¾ cup canned or cooked
   pumpkin
½ cup buttermilk
½ teaspoon vanilla extract
½ cup chopped walnuts

Sift together cake flour, soda, baking powder, salt, and spice. Cream shortening, gradually blending in sugars. Add eggs, one at a time, beating about 1 minute after each addition. Blend in pumpkin. Add sifted dry ingredients alternately with buttermilk and vanilla, beginning and ending with dry ingredients. Fold in nuts. Pour batter into two lightly greased and floured 8-inch layer cake pans. Bake at 350° for 25 to 30 minutes. Cool. Put layers together with Seafoam Frosting.

❧ Arkansas Blackberry Jam Cake

(THREE 9-INCH LAYER PANS)

3 cups sifted all-purpose flour
1 teaspoon soda
¼ teaspoon salt
1 teaspoon each: ground
   allspice, cloves, cinnamon,
   nutmeg
1 cup chopped pecans
1 cup candied citron or
   drained watermelon rind
   preserves, chopped

1 cup butter
1½ cups sugar
3 eggs, well beaten
1 cup blackberry jam
1 cup buttermilk

Sift together flour, soda, salt, and spices. Sift a little of the flour mixture over the nuts and citron. Cream butter until soft and smooth. Gradually add sugar and beat until light and fluffy. Beat in eggs and jam. Add flour mixture alternately with buttermilk. Beat after each addition until smooth. Fold in nuts and citron or watermelon rind. Pour into three 9-inch layer pans and bake at 350° for 20 to 25 minutes. Spread butter-sugar icing between layers and over cake.

❦ Holiday Jam Cake

(THREE 8-INCH LAYER PANS)

1 cup butter
1 cup sugar
1 cup blackberry jam
1 cup strawberry jam
1 cup fig preserves
5 egg yolks
1 tablespoon soda

1 cup buttermilk
3 cups all-purpose flour
1 tablespoon ground
  cinnamon
1 tablespoon ground allspice
5 egg whites, beaten
1 cup finely chopped pecans

Cream butter and sugar; add jam and preserves. Beat egg yolks well and add to first mixture, beating until smooth. Add soda to buttermilk and beat into first mixture alternately with flour, which has been sifted with spices. Beat egg whites until stiff and fold into batter along with the chopped pecans. Pour into three 8-inch, well-greased, layer cake pans and bake at 350° for 50 minutes or until cake tests done. Frost with Caramel Frosting.

❦ Jam Cake No. 1

(TWO 9-INCH LAYER PANS OR TUBE PAN)

⅓ cup butter or margarine
1 cup sugar
2 eggs
1 egg yolk
  Grated rind of 1 lemon
2¼ cups cake flour

2 teaspoons baking powder
1 teaspoon soda
½ teaspoon salt
1 cup sour milk
⅔ cup firm jam
½ cup chopped nuts

Cream butter and sugar until light and creamy. Beat in eggs and egg yolk, one at a time. Add lemon rind. Combine flour, baking powder, soda, and salt; add half of dry ingredients to creamed mixture. Beat in sour milk and jam. Add remaining dry ingredients. Beat after each addition until smooth. Fold in nuts. Bake in two greased 9-inch layer pans or a tube pan. Bake the layers for about 30 minutes; tube cake, for about 50 minutes at 350°.

❧ Jam Cake No. 2
(TWO 9-INCH LAYER PANS)

1 cup shortening
2 cups sugar
5 eggs, well beaten
3 cups all-purpose flour
½ teaspoon ground cinnamon
1½ teaspoons ground allspice
1½ teaspoons ground cloves

½ teaspoon salt
1 teaspoon soda
1 cup buttermilk
1 cup chopped dates or raisins
1 cup chopped nuts
1 cup jam (plum is good)

Cream shortening and sugar until light and fluffy. Add well-beaten eggs. Combine flour, spices, and salt. Dissolve soda in buttermilk. Add flour mixture and buttermilk alternately to creamed mixture, beginning and ending with flour mixture. Beat after each addition. Lightly dredge the fruit and nuts with a small amount of flour and add. Add jam. Stir just to get good distribution. Grease and line two 9-inch layer cake pans with paper and fill with batter. Bake at 325° for 40 minutes. Frost as you desire.

❧ Christmas Jam Cake
(THREE 9-INCH LAYER PANS)

2 cups sugar
1 cup butter or vegetable
  shortening
3 eggs
1 cup buttermilk
1 cup jam (any kind)

3 cups sifted cake flour
1 teaspoon soda
1 cup chopped nuts
1 cup chopped dates
1 cup raisins
1 apple, grated

Cream sugar and butter; add eggs and mix well. Combine buttermilk and jam. Add alternately with combined dry ingredients to the creamed mixture. Add nuts and fruits. Mix well. Bake in three greased 9-inch cake pans at 350° for 30 minutes. Turn out on racks to cool before frosting with Frosting for Jam Cake.

❧ Jellyroll No. 1
(15- x 10-INCH JELLYROLL PAN)

5 eggs, separated	2 tablespoons lemon juice
1 cup sugar	1 cup sifted cake flour
1 tablespoon grated lemon rind	¼ teaspoon salt
	1 cup jelly or jam

Beat egg whites until stiff, but not dry. Add half the sugar. Beat egg yolks until thick and lemon colored; add remaining sugar. Continue to beat until stiff enough to hold a peak; add lemon rind and juice. Fold gently into egg whites. Combine flour and salt and fold into egg mixture. Line 15- x 10-inch jellyroll pan with greased paper. Spread batter evenly. Bake at 350° for 15 minutes. Turn out on clean towel sprinkled with powdered sugar. Remove paper and trim crusts. Roll, beginning at 10-inch edge. Wrap in towel and cool. Unroll, spread with jelly or a lemon filling, and re-roll.

❧ Jellyroll No. 2
(15- x 10-INCH JELLYROLL PAN)

4 eggs	¼ teaspoon salt
¾ cup sugar	1 teaspoon vanilla extract
¾ cup sifted all-purpose flour	1 cup jelly or jam (any flavor)
¾ teaspoon baking powder	

Beat eggs until light. Add sugar gradually, and beat until mixture is thick and lemon colored. Sift dry ingredients together. Fold with vanilla into egg mixture. Turn into 15- x 10-inch jellyroll pan, lined with greased paper. Bake at 400° about 15 minutes, or until done. Cut crisp edges off cake. Turn pan at once onto a clean cloth sprinkled with powdered sugar.

Remove paper from cake. Spread cake with softened jelly or jam to within ½-inch of edges. Then roll it up quickly, starting at the narrow side of the cake. Finish with open edge on the under side. Wrap in towel and cool on rack.

❦ Cake-Mix Jellyroll

(15- x 10-inch jellyroll pan and 9- x 5- x 3-inch loaf pan)

1 box angel food cake mix
1 cup red jelly or cooked
   lemon filling

Mix cake as directed on box. Divide batter and spread half in 15- x 10-inch jellyroll pan which has been greased on bottom and lined with waxed paper and greased again. Spread batter evenly to corners. Bake at 375° for 15 to 20 minutes. Cool, loosen edges, and turn out on towel sprinkled with powdered sugar. Remove paper, roll cake in towel, starting with 10-inch side. Cool. Unroll cake and spread with whipped jelly or a lemon filling. Roll again and chill, seam side down. Bake remainder of cake in 9- x 5- x 3-inch loaf pan at 375° for 25 to 30 minutes.

❦ Chocolate Whipped Cream Roll

(15-inch jellyroll pan)

6 egg yolks
¾ cup sugar
5 tablespoons all-purpose
   flour
3 tablespoons cocoa
1 teaspoon baking powder

1 teaspoon hot water
6 egg whites
¼ cup sugar
1 pint heavy cream
   Powdered sugar

Beat egg yolks and ¾ cup sugar until light. Sift together flour, cocoa, and baking powder. Add to egg yolks and beat until smooth and well blended, then add hot water. Whip egg whites, add ¼ cup sugar and beat until stiff but not dry. Pour into greased paper-lined 15½- x 10½- x 1-inch jellyroll pan. Bake at 400° until cake leaves the sides of pan. Turn out on dry cloth which has been lightly coated with powdered sugar. Roll gently. Unroll, spread cream on cake and re-roll. Cover with Cooked Cream Icing.

☙ Lane Cake

(FOUR 9-INCH LAYER PANS)

1 cup butter	3½ teaspoons baking powder
2 cups sugar	¾ teaspoon salt
1 teaspoon vanilla extract	1 cup milk
3¼ cups all-purpose flour	8 egg whites, beaten

Cream butter until smooth; add sugar gradually and beat until light and fluffy. Add vanilla. Combine dry ingredients and add to creamed mixture alternately with milk, beating until smooth. Fold in beaten egg whites. Pour batter into four round 9-inch layer cake pans greased and lined on bottom with paper which has been greased. Bake at 375° for about 20 minutes. (If you have only two pans, bake half the batter at a time.) After removing cakes from oven, let stand 5 minutes; then turn out on racks to cool. Spread Lane Frosting between layers and on top and sides of cake. Cake is best if stored for several days before serving.

☙ Alabama Lane Cake

(FOUR 8-INCH LAYER PANS)

8 egg whites	3 teaspoons baking powder
1 cup butter or margarine	1 cup milk
2 cups sugar	1 teaspoon vanilla extract
3½ cups all-purpose flour	(optional)

Beat egg whites until they hold a peak, but are not dry. Set aside, then cream butter or margarine and sugar well. Sift flour and baking powder together and add to creamed mixture alternately with milk. Fold in beaten egg whites and vanilla. Bake in four 8-inch layers at 350° until brown. Fill with Filling for Lane Cake.

❧ Lemon Cake

(THREE 8- OR 9-INCH LAYER PANS)

¾ cup butter or margarine
1½ cups sugar
4 egg yolks, well beaten
1 teaspoon lemon extract
2½ cups all-purpose flour

1½ teaspoons baking powder
¼ teaspoon salt
¾ cup milk
4 egg whites, beaten

Cream the butter and sugar thoroughly and add the well-beaten egg yolks. Stir in the flavoring and add the dry ingredients alternately with the milk. Fold in the stiffly beaten egg whites. Bake in three well-greased 8- or 9-inch layer cake pans at 375° for about 25 minutes. Cool. Use Lemon Filling between layers. Top with Seven-Minute Frosting. Sprinkle with coconut, if desired.

❧ Lemon Gelatin Cake

(TUBE PAN)

1 package yellow cake mix
1 (3-ounce) package
    lemon-flavored gelatin

4 eggs
⅔ cup salad oil
⅔ cup water

Combine cake mix, lemon gelatin, eggs, salad oil, and water. Beat 10 minutes. Bake in greased tube pan at 350° about 1 to 1¼ hours.

❧ Lemon Supreme Special

(TUBE PAN)

1 box lemon cake mix
½ cup sugar
¾ cup cooking oil

1 cup apricot nectar
4 eggs

Mix cake mix, sugar, oil, and nectar together. Add eggs, one at a time. Bake in greased tube pan at 325° for 1 hour. Mix 1 cup powdered sugar and the juice of 1 lemon to make a glaze. Pour mixture over cake while cake is still warm.

❧ Lemon Jelly Cake
(THREE 9-INCH LAYER PANS)

⅓ cup butter	3 teaspoons baking powder
⅔ cup shortening	1 cup milk
2 cups sugar	6 egg whites, beaten
3½ cups sifted cake flour	1 teaspoon vanilla extract

Cream butter, shortening, and sugar until light and fluffy. Sift dry ingredients together and add alternately with milk. Fold in stiffly beaten egg whites and vanilla. Do not overbeat. Bake in three 9-inch layer pans at 375° about 25 minutes. Cool. Put layers together with Filling for Lemon Jelly Cake.

❧ Lemon-Date Cake
(TUBE PAN)

¾ cup shortening	1 cup buttermilk
1 cup sugar	1 teaspoon soda
2 eggs	2½ cups all-purpose flour
1 cup chopped pecans	1 teaspoon baking powder
1 (8-ounce) package dates	

Cream shortening and sugar together until light and fluffy; add eggs and beat well. Add pecans, chopped dates, and buttermilk in which soda has been dissolved. Add flour and baking powder which have been sifted together. Bake in a greased tube pan at 350° for 1 hour.

While cake is still hot, mix together the following and pour over it: 1 cup sugar and grated rind and juice of 2 large lemons. Let cool before cutting.

❧ Lemon-Cheese Cake
(THREE 8-INCH LAYER PANS)

1 cup butter or margarine	3 teaspoons baking powder
2 cups sugar	1 cup milk
4 eggs	1 teaspoon vanilla extract
3 cups all-purpose flour	

Cream butter or margarine and sugar and add beaten eggs. Fold in sifted dry ingredients alternately with milk. Bake in three greased 8- or 9-inch layer pans at 350° about 30 minutes.

❧ Lemon Chiffon Cake

(10-INCH TUBE PAN)

2 cups all-purpose flour	1 tablespoon grated lemon
1½ cups sugar	peel
3 teaspoons baking powder	7 egg yolks, unbeaten
1 teaspoon salt	½ teaspoon cream of tartar
½ cup salad oil	7 egg whites, beaten
¾ cup water	

Combine dry ingredients in large mixing bowl. Shape a well in center of flour mixture. Pour in the oil, water, lemon peel, and egg yolks. Beat until smooth.

In another large bowl, add cream of tartar to egg whites. Beat whites until they form very stiff peaks when beater is raised. Gradually pour egg yolk mixtures over the beaten whites, folding with rubber scraper until just blended. Pour batter into ungreased 10-inch tube pan. Bake at 325° for 55 minutes. Invert pan so top crust is air cooled. When cake is cold, loosen with spatula around edges.

❧ Lemon Extract Cake

(LOAF PANS)

1 pound butter or margarine	½ teaspoon salt
2⅓ cups sugar	½ pound candied cherries
6 eggs	¼ pound candied pineapple
3 ounces lemon extract	¼ pound white raisins
4 cups sifted all-purpose flour	1 pound (4 cups) shelled
1½ teaspoons baking powder	pecans

Cream butter or margarine and sugar. Add eggs and beat well. Add lemon extract and blend. Sift dry ingredients together and add to the creamed mixture. Chop fruits and nuts and add to cake mixture. Bake in loaf pans at 300° for 1½ to 2 hours.

❧ Chocolate Marble Cake

(TWO 8-INCH LAYER PANS)

3 cups sifted cake flour	1 teaspoon vanilla extract
2 teaspoons baking powder	6 egg whites, stiffly beaten
½ teaspoon salt	3 squares unsweetened
¾ cup butter or other	chocolate, melted
shortening	4 tablespoons sugar
2 cups sugar	¼ cup boiling water
¾ cup milk	½ teaspoon soda

Sift flour once, measure, add baking powder and salt, and sift together three times. Cream butter thoroughly, add sugar gradually, and cream together until light and fluffy. Add flour alternately with milk, beating after each addition until smooth. Add vanilla. Fold in egg whites. To melted chocolate, add sugar and boiling water, stirring until blended. Then add soda and stir until thickened. Cool slightly. Add to one-half of batter. Leave other half of batter plain. In two greased 8-inch layer cake pans, put alternate spoonfuls of dark and light mixtures until all is used. Bake at 350° for 35 minutes, or until done. Put Date Delight Filling between layers. Frost as desired.

If your family doesn't like date filling, use chocolate frosting and filling.

❧ Marble Cake

(TUBE PAN)

⅔ cup butter or margarine	1 cup milk
2 cups sugar	1 square unsweetened
4 eggs, well beaten	chocolate, melted and
3 cups all-purpose flour	cooled
4 teaspoons baking powder	1 teaspoon vanilla extract
½ teaspoon salt	

Cream the butter and sugar together; add the well-beaten eggs and mix well. Sift flour, baking powder, and salt; add alternately with milk to the first mixture. Put one-third of mixture into a bowl and add the melted chocolate. To the white batter, add the vanilla. Drop white batter, then chocolate, by spoonfuls into a well-greased tube pan. Bake at 350° for 1 hour. Cool 1 hour before removing from pan. Ice with a powdered sugar frosting, if desired.

❦ Modern Marble Cake
(8-INCH CAKE PAN)

½ cup shortening	½ teaspoon salt
1 cup sugar	½ cup milk
2 eggs, beaten	1 teaspoon vanilla extract
1¾ cups sifted cake flour	1 ounce (square) chocolate
2 teaspoons baking powder	2 tablespoons milk

Cream shortening with sugar until fluffy. Add beaten eggs. Add sifted dry ingredients and milk alternately in small amounts, beating well after each addition. Add vanilla. Divide batter into halves. Melt chocolate and add with 2 tablespoons milk to one half; blend well. Drop batter by tablespoons into greased pan, alternating white and chocolate. Bake at 350° for 50 to 60 minutes.

❦ Chocolate Marble Layer Cake
(TWO 8-INCH LAYER PANS)

1 square unsweetened chocolate, melted	¼ teaspoon salt
1 tablespoon sugar	6 tablespoons butter or other shortening
2 tablespoons hot water	1 cup sugar
¼ teaspoon soda	¾ cup milk
2 cups sifted cake flour	1 teaspoon vanilla extract
2 teaspoons baking powder	3 egg whites, beaten

To melted chocolate add 1 tablespoon sugar, hot water, and soda; blend. Cool. Sift flour once, measure, add baking powder and salt, and sift together three times. Cream shortening, add 1 cup sugar gradually and cream together until light and fluffy. Add flour alternately with milk, a small amount at a time, beating after each addition until smooth. Add vanilla. Beat egg whites until they will hold up in moist peaks. Stir quickly, but thoroughly into cake batter. Add chocolate mixture to one-third of batter. Put by tablespoons into two greased 8-inch layer pans, alternating light and dark mixtures. Then with knife cut carefully through batter once in a wide, zigzag course. Bake at 375° for 25 minutes, or until done. Spread Hungarian Chocolate Frosting between layers and on top and sides of cake.

❦ Molasses Layer Cake

(THREE 8-INCH LAYER PANS)

½ cup butter or margarine
½ cup sugar
1 cup unsulphured molasses
2 egg yolks
2½ cups self-rising flour
½ teaspoon salt
¼ teaspoon ground allspice

1 teaspoon ground cinnamon
¼ teaspoon ground cloves
½ cup milk
½ cup raisins
¾ cup chopped nuts
2 egg whites, stiffly beaten

Cream butter and sugar; add molasses and egg yolks and beat well. Combine flour, salt, and spices and add to creamed mixture alternately with milk, putting raisins and nuts in the last addition of flour mixture. Fold in stiffly beaten egg whites.

Put batter into three greased and floured 8-inch layer cake pans and bake at 350° about 25 minutes or until cake tests done. Put layers together with Molasses-Mocha Frosting. If frosting is desired for sides of cake, make 1½ times the recipe.

❦ Molasses Cake

(10-INCH TUBE PAN)

1 cup butter or margarine
1½ cups sugar
3 eggs
¾ cup unsulphured molasses
3¾ cups all-purpose flour
¾ teaspoon soda

¾ teaspoon salt
3 teaspoons ground cinnamon
1½ teaspoons ground cloves
1 teaspoon ground nutmeg
¾ cup buttermilk

Cream butter; slowly add sugar. Add eggs and beat until light and fluffy. Blend in molasses. Combine flour, soda, salt, and spices; add to creamed mixture alternately with buttermilk. Turn into a greased 10-inch tube pan. Bake at 325° for about 1 hour, or until cake tests done. Cool on wire rack. Serve with Lemon Topping, whipped cream, or ice cream.

❦ Molasses-Date Cake

(8-INCH TUBE PAN)

2¼ cups self-rising flour
1 cup sugar
1 cup molasses
1 cup butter, softened
2 eggs

1 teaspoon vanilla extract
1 cup chopped dates
1 cup chopped pecans
1 raw apple, grated

In a large mixing bowl combine flour, sugar, molasses, butter, eggs, and vanilla. Mix well at medium speed on electric mixer. When thoroughly blended, stir in dates, nuts, and grated apple. Spoon into a greased 8-inch tube cake pan and bake at 350° about 1 hour. Cake is done when it springs back if lightly touched in the center. Cool in pan about 5 minutes; then turn out on rack and cool completely. This is good served with ice cream or fruit cocktail. Yield: 10 servings.

❦ Nut Cream Cake

(TWO 8-INCH LAYER PANS)

4 egg whites
½ cup sugar
4 egg yolks
½ cup sugar
¼ teaspoon salt

½ cup vanilla wafer crumbs
 (about 10 wafers)
½ cup finely chopped pecans
 or walnuts
½ teaspoon baking powder

Beat egg whites until foamy white and double in volume. Use medium-size bowl. Beat in ½ cup sugar, 1 tablespoon at a time, beating well after each addition.

Beat egg yolks in large bowl; gradually beat in ½ cup sugar; stir in salt, wafer crumbs, nuts, and baking powder. Then fold in meringue until no streaks of white remain. Spread evenly in two well-greased 8-inch layer cake pans. Bake at 350° for 25 minutes, or until layers start to pull away from sides of pans. Cool on wire rack 10 minutes. Run knife around edges to loosen; turn out, cool completely. Put cake layers together on serving plate with Pudding Mix Frosting between and on top. Chill several hours or overnight in refrigerator. (The longer the better, for filling softens "cake.")

❧ Holiday Nut Cake

(9-INCH TUBE PAN)

3 cups sifted cake flour	1 egg yolk, unbeaten
2 teaspoons baking powder	¾ cup milk
¾ teaspoon salt	1 teaspoon orange extract
1 cup butter	1 teaspoon almond extract
1¾ cups sugar	¾ to 1 cup very finely chopped
3 eggs, unbeaten	or ground nuts

Measure flour; add baking powder, and salt; sift three times. Cream butter, add sugar, and cream together until light and fluffy. Add eggs and egg yolk and beat thoroughly. Then add flour alternately with milk, a small amount at a time, beating after each addition until smooth. Add flavorings and nuts, and mix well.

Pour batter into 9-inch tube pan which has been greased and lightly floured. Bake at 375° for 1 hour, or until wire tester comes out clean and dry. Cool before removing from pan.

You may also use two 9- x 5- x 3-inch loaf pans lined on bottoms with oiled paper. Bake at 325° for about 1 hour.

❧ Christmas Pecan Cake

(10-INCH TUBE PAN)

2 cups (1 pound) butter or	1 tablespoon vanilla extract
margarine	4 cups chopped pecans
2 cups sugar	1½ cups golden raisins
6 eggs	3 cups sifted all-purpose flour
1 tablespoon lemon juice	¼ teaspoon salt
1 teaspoon grated lemon peel	1 teaspoon baking powder

Cream butter and sugar until fluffy. Beat in eggs, one at a time. Add lemon juice, peel, and vanilla. Mix nuts and raisins with ¼ cup flour. Sift remaining dry ingredients. Alternately fold nuts and raisins and dry ingredients into creamed mixture. Spoon into a greased paper-lined 10-inch tube pan; bake at 300° about 1 hour and 50 minutes. Cool; then remove from pan. Yield: 10-inch cake.

Variation: For a sweeter, more moist cake, pour a syrup of ¼ cup each orange juice, lemon juice, and sugar over cake while it's hot. Pan may be lined with foil. Flavor improves in the freezer.

❦ Pecan-Date Loaf

(9½- x 5½- x 2½-INCH LOAF PAN)

1 pound whole pitted dates	4 egg yolks
1 pound pecan halves	½ cup sugar
1 cup sifted all-purpose flour	½ cup dark corn syrup
½ teaspoon salt	4 egg whites
2 teaspoons baking powder	2 teaspoons vanilla extract

In a large bowl place whole dates, pecan halves, flour, salt, and baking powder. Mix together with a spoon so that dates and nuts are well coated.

In a smaller bowl beat egg yolks until creamy, add sugar, beat until thick, and stir in corn syrup. Pour into date-pecan mixture and stir well. Fold in stiffly beaten egg whites. Add vanilla and spoon into well-greased and floured 9½- x 5½- x 2½-inch loaf pan. Bake at 325° for 1 to 1¼ hours or until cake tester is clean.

❦ Pecan Cake No. 1

(TUBE PAN)

1 stick butter or margarine	2 cups sifted all-purpose flour
2 cups sugar	1½ pounds (6 cups) shelled
4 eggs	pecans
2 squares unsweetened chocolate, melted and cooled	

Cream butter; add sugar and beat until smooth. Add eggs, one at a time, beating well after each addition. Add cooled chocolate and mix well. Sift flour and mix with pecans. Pour batter into flour and pecans and mix well.

Grease tube pan and line with heavy brown paper that has been oiled (this is the secret of the cake; paper must be very heavy). Cover top of cake with oiled paper. Bake at 250° for 2 to 3 hours, or until cake tests done.

Cake may also be baked in large loaf pan and two smaller ones; doubled recipe will fill three large loaf pans.

❦ Pecan Cake No. 2

(TUBE PAN)

1 cup butter	1 cup sweet milk or whiskey
2½ cups sugar	or some of each
3½ cups all-purpose flour	1 quart pecan meats
2 teaspoons baking powder	1 pound raisins
1 teaspoon salt	Spices to suit

Cream butter and sugar. Add dry ingredients alternately with milk. Stir in pecans, raisins, and spices. Put in greased and floured tube pan and bake at 275° for 3 to 4 hours or until done. Frost with caramel frosting.

❦ Texas Pecan Cake

(10-INCH TUBE PAN)

2 cups butter or margarine	1½ teaspoons baking powder
2 cups sugar	2 cups white raisins
6 eggs, well beaten	4 cups pecan halves,
1 tablespoon lemon extract	unbroken
4 cups all-purpose flour	

Cream butter or margarine and sugar; add well-beaten eggs and lemon extract. Add flour and baking powder, which have been sifted together, with raisins and pecans mixed in. Blend well and pour into a 10-inch tube pan and bake at 275° for 2 hours.

❦ Rich Pecan Cake

(TUBE PAN)

4 eggs	1 teaspoon baking powder
2 cups sugar	1 teaspoon soda
1 cup shortening (butter,	1 teaspoon ground cinnamon
margarine, lard, or	½ teaspoon ground cloves
hydrogenated fat)	1 cup buttermilk or sour milk
3 cups all-purpose flour	2 cups chopped pecans

Beat eggs; add sugar and shortening. Add dry ingredients and milk alternately, and beat with electric beater. Add pecans. Bake in a greased tube pan at 350° for 1 hour.

❦ Pecan-Raisin Cake

(10-INCH TUBE PAN)

2 cups butter	3 cups all-purpose flour
2 cups sugar	¼ teaspoon salt
6 eggs	1 teaspoon baking powder
1 tablespoon lemon juice	2 cups golden raisins
1 tablespoon vanilla extract	4 cups chopped pecans

Cream butter and sugar until fluffy. Beat in eggs, one at a time. Add lemon juice and vanilla. Combine 2½ cups flour, salt, and baking powder and add to creamed mixture. Mix raisins and nuts with ½ cup flour. Add to creamed mixture. Spoon into greased paper-lined 10-inch tube pan or two loaf pans. Bake at 350° for about 1 hour, or until cake tests done.

❦ Black Walnut-Spice Cake

(THREE 9-INCH LAYER PANS)

1 cup black walnut meats	½ teaspoon ground cinnamon
½ cup shortening	½ teaspoon ground nutmeg
2 cups brown sugar	½ teaspoon ground cloves
3 egg yolks, well beaten	1 teaspoon baking powder
3 cups all-purpose flour	¾ cup milk
½ teaspoon salt	3 egg whites

Place shelled black walnuts in boiling water a few minutes, then drain and set aside. Cream shortening and sugar, and add well-beaten egg yolks. Sift together dry ingredients and add alternately with milk to the creamed mixture. Add nutmeats. Fold in well-beaten egg whites. Bake in three greased 9-inch layer pans at 350° about 20 minutes, or until lightly browned. Top with a caramel frosting.

❦ Black Walnut Cake

(TUBE PAN)

½ cup butter
2 cups brown sugar
3 egg yolks, beaten
2 cups all-purpose flour
3 teaspoons baking powder
½ teaspoon salt

⅔ cup milk
1 teaspoon vanilla extract
1 cup black walnuts, chopped
  fine or ground
3 egg whites, beaten

Cream butter; add sugar and beat until smooth. Add beaten egg yolks and mix well. Combine dry ingredients and add to creamed mixture alternately with milk. Add vanilla and walnuts and mix well. Fold in stiffly beaten egg whites.

Bake in greased tube pan at 350° for 45 minutes.

❦ Walnut Cake

(TWO 8-INCH LAYER PANS)

2 cups cake flour
½ teaspoon salt
2½ teaspoons baking powder
½ cup shortening
1¼ cups sugar
2 eggs, separated
⅓ cup milk
1 teaspoon lemon juice

⅓ cup maraschino cherry
  syrup (drained from
  cherries)
1 (5-ounce) bottle maraschino
  cherries (chop all but five)
½ cup chopped walnuts
⅛ teaspoon salt
  Walnut halves
  White frosting

Sift flour, salt, and baking powder twice. Cream shortening and sugar and stir in egg yolks and mix well. Add liquids and dry ingredients alternately to creamed mixture. Fold in stiffly beaten egg whites. Add chopped cherries (floured) to half the batter; add chopped walnuts (floured) and ⅛ teaspoon extra salt to the other half of the batter. Bake in two greased 8-inch square pans at 375° about 25 minutes. Frost with a white frosting and decorate with walnut halves and five cherries.

❦ Black Walnut Layer Cake

(TWO 9-INCH LAYER PANS)

⅔ cup shortening	2¾ teaspoons baking powder
1½ cups sugar	¼ teaspoon salt
1 teaspoon vanilla extract	¾ cup milk
3 egg yolks, beaten	1 cup ground black walnuts
2 cups all-purpose flour	3 egg whites, beaten

Cream shortening, sugar, and vanilla until fluffy. Add beaten egg yolks and beat thoroughly. Add dry ingredients alternately with milk in a small amount. Add nuts, and fold in stiffly beaten egg whites. Put batter in two greased 9-inch pans. Bake at 350° for 30 minutes. Frost with Black Walnut Frosting.

❦ Orange Slice Cake

(13- x 9- x 2-INCH PAN)

1 cup butter or margarine	1 pound candy orange slices, chopped
2 cups sugar	2 cups chopped nuts
4 eggs	1 can flaked coconut
1 teaspoon soda	1 cup fresh orange juice
½ cup buttermilk	2 cups powdered sugar
3½ cups all-purpose flour	
1 pound dates, chopped	

Cream butter or margarine and sugar until smooth. Add eggs, one at a time, and beat well after each addition. Dissolve soda in buttermilk and add to creamed mixture. Place flour in large bowl and add dates, orange slices, and nuts. Stir to coat each piece.

Add flour mixture and coconut to creamed mixture. This makes a very stiff dough that should be mixed with the hands. Put in a greased and floured 13- x 9- x 2-inch cake pan. Bake at 250° for 2½ to 3 hours. Combine orange juice and powdered sugar and pour over hot cake. Let stand in pan overnight.

❦ Orange Cake No. 1

(TWO 9-INCH LAYER PANS)

2½ cups sifted cake flour	¾ teaspoon salt
3 teaspoons baking powder	1 tablespoon grated orange
⅓ cup orange juice	rind
2 tablespoons lemon juice	1½ cups sugar
⅔ cup shortening	3 eggs, unbeaten

Sift cake flour and baking powder together three times. Combine fruit juices and add enough water to make 1 cup liquid. Combine shortening, salt, and grated orange rind. Add sugar gradually, and cream well. Add flour and liquid mixture alternately, in small amounts, lightly folding in each addition. Bake in two greased 9-inch layer cake pans at 375° for 25 to 30 minutes. Spread Orange Filling between layers. Cover top and sides with a boiled frosting or Seven-Minute Frosting flavored with grated orange rind.

❦ Orange Cake No. 2

(THREE 9-INCH LAYER PANS)

1 cup butter	3 cups sifted cake flour
2 cups sugar	9 egg whites (beaten stiff)
1 cup milk	1 teaspoon lemon juice
2 teaspoons baking powder	

Cream the butter. Add sugar. Beat well. Add milk. Sift baking powder with flour and add alternately to creamed mixture with the beaten egg whites. Add lemon juice. Mix all lightly. Bake in three 9- or 10-inch greased layer pans at 350° for 1 hour. Spread layers with Orange Filling and cover the top with a boiled frosting flavored with 4 tablespoons orange juice.

℘ Orange-Date Cake

(TUBE PAN)

1 cup butter or margarine	1 teaspoon soda
2 cups sugar	½ teaspoon salt
4 eggs	1⅓ cups buttermilk
2 tablespoons grated orange	½ cup sifted cake flour
rind	1 cup chopped dates
1 teaspoon vanilla extract	1 cup chopped pecans
3½ cups sifted cake flour	

Cream butter or margarine, add sugar, and cream until smooth. Blend in eggs, one at a time. Add orange rind and vanilla. Sift dry ingredients, measure, and sift together. Add to creamed mixture alternately with the buttermilk. Then mix the ½ cup flour, dates, and nuts, and fold into cake mixture. Turn into greased tube pan. Bake at 350° for 1½ hours.

℘ Orange Mist Cake

(10-INCH TUBE PAN)

10 egg yolks	1 cup plus 2 tablespoons sifted
1 cup plus 2 tablespoons sugar	all-purpose flour
¼ cup orange juice	½ teaspoon salt
1 tablespoon grated orange	1 teaspoon cream of tartar
rind	10 egg whites

Beat egg yolks well. Add all but ⅔ cup sugar slowly to yolks, beating well. Slowly add orange juice, rind, flour, and remaining sugar. Mix well. Add salt and cream of tartar to egg whites; whip until stiff. Fold into yolk mixture. Pour into ungreased 10-inch tube pan. Bake at 300° for 1 hour. Cool and cut into three layers. Frost with Orange Cloud Frosting.

❦ Easy Cake-Pineapple Filling

(THREE 8-INCH LAYER PANS)

⅔ cup shortening
2 cups sugar
4 eggs
3 cups all-purpose flour
3 teaspoons baking powder
⅛ teaspoon salt

1 cup water
1 teaspoon vanilla extract
1 teaspoon lemon juice
   Pineapple Filling
   White frosting

Cream shortening and sugar until smooth. Add eggs, one at a time, beating after each addition. Sift dry ingredients together and add to creamed mixture alternately with water. Stir in vanilla and lemon juice. Bake in three greased and floured 8-inch pans at 350° for 25 minutes or until cake tests done. Cool. Put Pineapple Filling between layers; frost with favorite white frosting.

Pineapple Filling

1 tall can crushed pineapple,
   drained

2 tablespoons flour
½ cup sugar

Combine ingredients in a saucepan. Cook until thick; stir constantly. Cool; spread between layers.

❦ Pineapple Loaf Cake

(10-INCH TUBE PAN)

3 sticks margarine
1½ boxes powdered sugar
6 eggs
1 teaspoon vanilla extract
1 teaspoon lemon juice

1 sugar box of all-purpose
   flour
1 No. 2½ can crushed pineapple
   (well drained)

Cream margarine; add sugar and beat well. Add eggs, one at a time, beating well after each addition. Add vanilla and lemon juice. Stir in flour and mix well. Add pineapple (be sure that all juice has been drained). Spoon batter into a greased and floured 10-inch tube pan. Bake at 350° for 1½ hours or until cake tests done. No frosting is needed for this cake; it keeps well.

❦ Pineapple Spice Cake

(TUBE PAN)

2 cups sugar
1¼ cups salad oil
4 egg yolks
4 tablespoons hot water
½ teaspoon salt
2 teaspoons ground cinnamon
1 small can (1 cup) crushed
    pineapple

2½ cups all-purpose flour
2 teaspoons baking powder
1 teaspoon ground nutmeg
4 egg whites, beaten
1 cup chopped pecans

Combine all ingredients except egg whites and pecans. Mix well. Fold in beaten egg whites and pecans. Pour batter in a greased tube pan. Bake at 350° for 1¼ hours.

❦ Pineapple Layer Cake

(THREE 9-INCH LAYER PANS)

1 cup shortening
2 cups sugar
4 egg yolks, beaten
1 teaspoon vanilla extract
½ teaspoon lemon extract
2 to 4 drops almond extract
½ teaspoon soda

1⅓ cups crushed pineapple, not
    drained
3½ cups all-purpose flour
3 teaspoons baking powder
½ teaspoon salt
4 egg whites, beaten

Cream shortening and sugar until light and fluffy. Add egg yolks and flavoring and beat well. Stir soda into pineapple and add to creamed mixture. Combine flour and baking powder. Add to creamed mixture and beat until smoothly blended. Add salt to egg whites and beat until stiff; fold into mixture. Put batter in three greased and floured 9-inch cake pans. Bake at 350° about 30 to 35 minutes. Cool and frost as desired.

❧ Pound Cake

(10-INCH TUBE PAN)

4½ cups sifted cake flour	2½ teaspoons vanilla extract
2 teaspoons double-acting baking powder	¼ teaspoon ground mace
1 teaspoon salt	8 eggs
2 cups butter	½ cup milk
2½ cups sugar	Orange Butter Glaze
	Flaked coconut

Sift flour with baking powder and salt. Cream butter 10 minutes or until *very soft and fluffy*. Add sugar, 2 tablespoons at a time, creaming thoroughly after each addition. Blend in vanilla and mace. Thoroughly beat in eggs, one at a time. Add flour mixture alternately with milk, beginning and ending with flour and beating after each addition until smooth. Bake in a greased and floured 10-inch tube pan at 325° for about 1½ hours or until cake tester inserted into cake comes out clean. Cool in pan 15 minutes; remove and finish cooling on rack. Glaze top and drizzle down sides of cake with Orange Butter Glaze. Sprinkle with flaked coconut.

Note: Cake is easier to slice when wrapped tightly in plastic wrap or aluminum foil and stored overnight.

Orange-Butter Glaze

2 tablespoons orange juice	2½ cups sifted powdered sugar
1 tablespoon milk	½ teaspoon grated orange rind
1 tablespoon butter	(optional)

Heat orange juice, milk, and butter until butter melts. Add to sugar in a small bowl; then beat until smooth. Add rind. Increase liquid if thinner consistency is desired. Yield: ¾ cup.

❧ Old-Fashioned Pound Cake

(9-INCH TUBE PAN)

2 cups all-purpose flour	1⅔ cups sifted sugar
1 cup butter (decreased by 1 tablespoon if other shortening used)	5 eggs
	1 teaspoon vanilla extract

Sift flour, measure, and sift again five times. Cream butter, add sugar, and beat until no sugar grains appear. Then add one egg and beat until no egg can be seen; then another, and proceed as before. When the last egg has been added, beat long and hard. Add the flour, beat again, and when it becomes a creamy mass, add vanilla. Put in greased and floured 9-inch tube pan. Bake at 275° for 1 hour, or until done.

One-Two-Three-Four Pound Cake

(TUBE PAN)

1 cup shortening	3 cups all-purpose flour
2 cups sugar	½ teaspoon soda
4 eggs	½ teaspoon salt
2 teaspoons vanilla extract	1 cup buttermilk

Cream shortening and sugar. Add eggs, one at a time, and beat between each addition. Add vanilla and then alternately add the dry ingredients and buttermilk. Put batter in a greased tube pan. Bake at 325° until light golden brown, about 1¼ hours.

Dark Secret Pound Cake

(TUBE OR BUNDT PAN)

1 (6-ounce) package semi-sweet chocolate pieces	⅔ cup soft butter or margarine
2½ cups sifted all-purpose flour	3 eggs, unbeaten
1 teaspoon soda	⅔ cup buttermilk
1 teaspoon salt	1 teaspoon vanilla extract
1 cup sugar	½ cup chopped walnuts

Melt chocolate pieces over hot (not boiling) water. Remove from heat; cool. Sift together flour, soda and salt; set aside. Combine sugar and butter and beat until creamy. Blend in chocolate. Add eggs, one at a time, beating well after each addition. Stir in flour mixture alternately with buttermilk and vanilla combined. Add chopped walnuts. Pour batter into greased tube or Bundt pan. Bake at 350° about 1 hour and 10 minutes. While cake is hot, decorate with candied cherries, angelica, almonds, etc., if desired.

❧ Buttermilk Pound Cake No. 1

(10-INCH TUBE PAN)

1 cup vegetable shortening	6 eggs
3 cups sugar	3 cups all-purpose flour
1½ teaspoons vanilla or lemon extract	¼ teaspoon salt
	1 cup buttermilk

Cream shortening and sugar. Add flavoring. Add eggs, one at a time, beating well after each addition. Sift dry ingredients together and add to creamed mixture alternately with buttermilk. Spoon batter into greased 10-inch tube pan and bake at 325° for 1¼ hours or until cake tests done.

❧ Buttermilk Pound Cake No. 2

(LOAF PAN)

1 cup shortening	3 cups all-purpose flour
2 cups sugar	¾ teaspoon salt
4 eggs	½ teaspoon soda
1 teaspoon vanilla extract	½ teaspoon baking powder
1 teaspoon orange flavoring	1 cup buttermilk

Cream shortening and sugar until light and fluffy. Add eggs and beat well. Add vanilla and orange flavoring. Sift dry ingredients together three times. Add dry ingredients to creamed mixture alternately with buttermilk. Spoon into greased loaf pan and bake at 300° about 1 hour.

❧ Brown Sugar Pound Cake

(TUBE PAN)

1 cup shortening	½ teaspoon salt
1 stick margarine	½ teaspoon baking powder
1 box light brown sugar, sifted	1 cup evaporated milk
5 eggs	2 teaspoons maple flavoring
3 cups all-purpose flour	Brown Sugar Frosting

Cream shortening, margarine, and sifted brown sugar. Add eggs, one at a time, beating well after each addition. Sift dry ingredients and add them alternately with milk. Add flavoring. Pour mixture into greased and floured tube pan; bake at 300° for 1½ hours. Cover with Brown Sugar Frosting.

❧ Pound Cake With Apricot Brandy
(LARGE TUBE PAN)

2 sticks margarine
3 cups sugar
6 eggs
3 cups all-purpose flour
½ teaspoon salt
¼ teaspoon soda
1 cup commercial sour cream

½ teaspoon lemon extract
1 teaspoon orange extract
¼ teaspoon almond extract
½ teaspoon rum extract
1 teaspoon vanilla extract
½ cup apricot brandy

Cream margarine and sugar until light and fluffy. Add eggs, one at a time, beating well after each addition. Sift dry ingredients together and add to creamed mixture. Combine sour cream with extracts and brandy; add to cake batter and mix well. Bake in a large well-greased and floured tube pan (or Bundt pan and loaf pan) at 325° for 70 minutes. Let cool in pan before removing.

❧ Infallible Pound Cake
(10-INCH TUBE PAN)

1½ cups vegetable shortening
2½ cups sugar
8 eggs
3 cups all-purpose flour

1 teaspoon lemon extract
1 teaspoon vanilla extract
1 teaspoon almond extract

Cream shortening and sugar until smooth. Add eggs, one at a time, beating well after each addition. Add flour, stir well, then add flavorings. Bake in a greased tube pan at 325° for 1½ hours.

❧ Chocolate Pound Cake No. 1

(10-INCH TUBE PAN)

3 squares unsweetened chocolate	1 cup butter or margarine
2⅓ cups all-purpose flour	⅔ cup milk
¾ teaspoon cream of tartar	1 teaspoon vanilla extract
½ teaspoon soda	3 eggs
1½ teaspoons salt	1 egg yolk
1¾ cups sugar	

Melt chocolate over hot (not boiling) water. Sift the flour, cream of tartar, soda, salt, and sugar together. Work the butter or margarine to the very soft, creamy stage and add cooled chocolate. Stir in small portions of the sifted dry ingredients, blending thoroughly. (Mixture will be very crumbly looking at this stage.) Stir in milk and vanilla until flour is dampened. Beat 300 strokes by hand or 2 minutes at low speed on electric mixer. Add unbeaten eggs and yolk to batter and beat 150 more strokes or 1 minute longer with electric mixer. Pour into a 10-inch tube pan which has been lined in the bottom with waxed paper. Bake at 350° for 60 to 70 minutes, or until cake tester comes out dry. Let cool in pan for 15 minutes, then loosen sides with a spatula, invert pan on cooling rack, and cool completely.

❧ Chocolate Pound Cake No. 2

(10-INCH TUBE PAN)

1 cup butter or margarine	½ teaspoon baking powder
½ cup shortening	½ teaspoon salt
3 cups sugar	4 tablespoons cocoa (may be
5 eggs	heaping, if desired)
1 teaspoon vanilla extract	1 cup milk
3 cups all-purpose flour	

Cream together butter and shortening. Add sugar. Add eggs, one at a time, beating after each addition. Add vanilla. Combine dry ingredients and add alternately with milk to creamed mixture. Bake in greased 10-inch tube pan at 325° for 1 hour and 20 minutes.

❧ Chocolate Pound Cake No. 3

(LARGE TUBE PAN)

½ pound margarine	2 teaspoons baking powder
½ cup vegetable shortening	½ cup cocoa
3 cups sugar	½ teaspoon salt
5 eggs	1¼ cups milk
3 cups all-purpose flour	1 tablespoon vanilla extract

Cream margarine and shortening, adding sugar gradually. Add eggs, one at a time, beating well after each addition. Sift together the flour, baking powder, cocoa, and salt. Add to creamed mixture alternately with the milk. Add vanilla. Pour batter into a large tube pan that has been greased and dusted with flour. Bake at 325° for 1½ hours.

❧ Sweet Chocolate Pound Cake

(TUBE PAN)

1 (¼-pound) package sweet cooking chocolate	1 cup butter or margarine
2¾ cups all-purpose flour	1¾ cups sugar
1¼ teaspoons baking powder	4 eggs, unbeaten
½ teaspoon salt	1 teaspoon vanilla extract
	1 cup milk

Heat chocolate over hot water until partially melted. Remove from hot water and stir rapidly until entirely melted; cool. Meanwhile, measure sifted flour, add baking powder and salt, and sift together. Cream butter until softened; gradually add sugar, creaming after each addition until mixture is very light and fluffy. This takes about 10 minutes with an electric mixer and longer by hand. Add eggs, one at a time, beating well with each addition. Stir in cooled chocolate and vanilla. Beat well. Alternately add flour and milk, beating with each addition until batter is smooth. Pour into tube pan which has been lined on bottom with paper and greased around the tube and sides. Bake at 325° for 1 hour and 30 to 35 minutes. Cool cake in pan 15 minutes, then loosen from the tube and sides with a knife. Remove from pan and cool. Frost, if desired.

❧ German's Chocolate Pound Cake
(9-INCH TUBE PAN)

2 cups sugar
1 cup shortening
4 eggs
2 teaspoons butter flavoring
2 teaspoons vanilla extract
1 cup buttermilk

3 cups sifted all-purpose flour
½ teaspoon soda
1 teaspoon salt
1 (4-ounce) package sweet
   chocolate, softened

Cream sugar and shortening until light and fluffy. Add eggs, flavorings, and buttermilk and mix well. Sift flour, soda, and salt together; stir into creamed mixture. Blend in chocolate. Pour into a greased and floured 9-inch tube pan. Bake at 300° for 1½ hours. Place under tight-fitting cake cover while still hot; leave covered until cool

❧ Dolley Madison Pound Cake
(LARGE TUBE PAN)

1 pound butter
1 pound granulated sugar
12 eggs, separated and beaten
1 pound all-purpose flour,
   sifted twice

½ pound pitted dates
12 almonds, skinned
6 tablespoons honey

Cream the butter and sugar together. Add well-beaten egg yolks and stiffly beaten egg whites alternately with flour to the creamed sugar-butter mixture. Beat. When very light, pour into a well-greased and floured round pan. The pan should be large enough to hold the entire mixture to within an inch or more at the top of the pan. Bake at 350° until golden brown. Baking should be slow and watched carefully. Allow to cool while in the pan. When cooled, remove from pan and decorate with dates and almonds. Pour honey over the top for glaze.

Lemon Pound Cake

(TUBE PAN)

2 cups butter or margarine
2 cups sugar
6 eggs
4 cups sifted all-purpose flour
1 pound white raisins
  (dredged in a little flour)
4 cups chopped pecans
1 (2-ounce) bottle lemon
  flavoring

Cream butter or margarine and sugar well. Add one egg at a time, then flour, then raisins, and last nuts and flavoring. Bake in paper-lined greased tube pan at 325° for 1½ hours.

Pineapple Pound Cake

(10-INCH TUBE PAN)

½ cup vegetable shortening
½ pound butter or margarine
  (2 sticks)
2¾ cups sugar
6 large eggs
3 cups sifted all-purpose flour
1 teaspoon baking powder
¼ cup milk
1 teaspoon vanilla extract
¾ cup undrained crushed
  pineapple and juice
¼ cup butter or margarine
  (½ stick)
1½ cups powdered sugar
1 cup crushed pineapple,
  drained

Cream shortening, butter, and sugar. Add eggs, one at a time, beating thoroughly after each addition. Add flour sifted with baking powder, 1 spoonful at a time, alternately with milk. Add vanilla; stir in crushed pineapple and juice and blend well. Pour batter into well-greased 10-inch tube pan.

Place in cold oven. Turn oven to 325° and bake for 1½ hours or until top springs back when touched lightly. Let stand for few minutes in pan. Run knife around edges and remove carefully to rack.

Combine butter, powdered sugar, and about 1 cup drained pineapple. Pour over cake while hot.

❦ Sweet Potato Pound Cake

(10-INCH TUBE PAN)

1 cup butter or margarine
2 cups sugar
2½ cups mashed cooked sweet
    potatoes
4 eggs
3 cups all-purpose flour
¼ teaspoon salt
2 teaspoons baking powder

1 teaspoon soda
½ teaspoon ground nutmeg
1 teaspoon ground cinnamon
1 teaspoon vanilla extract
½ cup chopped nuts
½ cup flaked coconut
Icing

Cream butter and sugar; add potatoes and beat until mixture is light and fluffy. Add eggs, one at a time, beating well after each addition. Combine flour, salt, baking powder, soda, nutmeg, and cinnamon; stir into creamed mixture. Add vanilla and mix well. Stir in nuts and coconut. Spoon mixture into a greased 10-inch tube pan and bake at 350° for 1¼ hours or until cake tests done. While cake is still hot, spread with Icing, if desired.

Icing

Grated rind of 1 orange
Juice and grated rind of 1
    lemon

1 box powdered sugar

Mix well; spread over hot Sweet Potato Pound Cake.

❦ Coconut Pound Cake No. 1

(10-INCH TUBE PAN)

2 sticks butter or margarine
½ cup vegetable shortening
3 cups sugar
6 eggs
½ teaspoon almond flavoring

1 teaspoon coconut flavoring
3 cups all-purpose flour
1 cup milk
1 (7-ounce) can flaked
    coconut

Cream butter, shortening, and sugar until light and fluffy. Add eggs, one at a time, beating well after each addition. Add flavorings and mix well. Alternately add flour and milk, beating after each addition. Stir in coconut. Spoon batter into 10-inch greased tube pan or Bundt pan. Bake at 350° for 1¼ hours.

❦ Coconut Pound Cake No. 2

(TUBE PAN)

1 cup vegetable shortening
2 cups sugar
1 teaspoon vanilla extract
1 teaspoon butter flavoring
6 eggs

2 cups all-purpose flour
1 teaspoon salt
1 (7-ounce) can flaked
   coconut
Glaze

Cream shortening and sugar until light and fluffy. Add flavorings and mix well. Add eggs, one at a time, beating well after each addition. Sift flour and salt together and add to creamed mixture. Fold in coconut. Bake in a well-greased and floured tube pan at 325° for about 1 hour and 10 minutes or until cake tests done. Add Glaze.

Glaze

1½ cups sugar
¾ cup boiling water

3 teaspoons coconut flavoring

Mix all three ingredients together; bring to a boil and boil for 1 minute. Pour three-fourths of the mixture over the baked cake; return cake to 325° oven for 3 minutes. Remove cake from oven, turn out on cake plate, and pour remaining glaze over cake.

❦ Favorite Date-Nut Pound Cake

(10-INCH TUBE PAN)

1 pound butter
2 cups sugar
6 eggs
1 (1-ounce) bottle lemon
   extract

4 cups all-purpose flour,
   divided
1 pound dates, chopped
1 pound (4 cups) pecans and
   walnuts, chopped fine

Cream butter well; add sugar and continue beating until smooth and fluffy. Add eggs, one at a time, beating well after each addition. Add flavoring. Sprinkle 1 cup flour over dates and nuts. Add 3 cups flour to creamed mixture; mix well. Add dates and nuts and spoon into a well-greased and floured 10-inch tube cake pan. Bake at 300° for 2 hours. Remove from oven and turn it upside down for a few minutes.

🍂 Sour Cream Pound Cake

(TUBE PAN)

½ pound butter	½ pint commercial sour cream
3 cups sugar	¼ teaspoon soda
6 egg yolks, beaten	6 egg whites, beaten
3 cups all-purpose flour	1 teaspoon vanilla extract
Pinch salt	1 teaspoon almond extract

Cream butter and sugar. Add egg yolks. Sift flour three times with salt. Add alternately with the cream to which soda has been added. Fold in stiffly beaten egg whites, vanilla, and almond flavoring. Put batter in greased and lightly floured tube pan and bake at 300° for 1½ hours.

🍂 Cake Mix–Poppy Seed Cake

(TWO 8-INCH LAYER PANS)

⅓ cup poppy seeds	1 package white cake mix

Soak poppy seeds 1 hour in total amount of liquid required by directions on cake mix package. Then prepare cake mix according to package directions, using poppy seed mixture in place of milk or water. Bake in two 8-inch layers, as directed. Cool and frost with Lemon Butter Cream Frosting.

🍂 Poppy Seed Cake No. 1

(TWO 9-INCH LAYER PANS)

½ cup poppy seeds	¾ cup margarine
1 cup milk	1¼ cups sugar
2½ cups sifted all-purpose flour	4 egg whites
2½ teaspoons baking powder	1 teaspoon vanilla extract
½ teaspoon salt	

Add poppy seeds to milk and soak in refrigerator overnight. Sift together flour, baking powder, and salt. Cream margarine, add sugar gradually until light and fluffy. Add sifted dry ingredients alternately with poppy seed mixture. Beat egg whites until frothy. Add remaining ½ cup sugar gradually to egg whites, beating until stiff. Fold beaten egg white-sugar mixture into batter. Add vanilla. Pour into two greased 9-inch layer cake pans lined with waxed paper. Bake at 350° for 25 to 30 minutes. Cool; spread Custard Filling between layers and Chocolate Frosting on top.

❦ Poppy Seed Cake No. 2

(TWO 8-INCH LAYER PANS)

⅓ cup poppy seeds
½ cup water
¾ cup shortening
1½ cups sugar
2¼ cups sifted cake flour

2 teaspoons baking powder
½ teaspoon salt
1 cup water
4 egg whites, stiffly beaten

Soak poppy seeds in half-cup water. Cream shortening and sugar until smooth. Combine dry ingredients and add creamed mixture alternately with 1 cup water. Fold in stiffly beaten egg whites. Drain poppy seeds and add to creamed mixture. Put batter in two greased 8-inch layer cake pans. Bake at 350° for 30 minutes.

❦ Mashed Potato Cake

(TUBE PAN)

2 cups brown sugar
1 cup butter
4 eggs, beaten
½ cup cooked mashed potatoes
2 cups all-purpose flour
2 teaspoons baking powder
½ teaspoon salt

1 teaspoon ground cinnamon
½ teaspoon ground cloves
1 teaspoon ground nutmeg
1 cup milk
1 square unsweetened
  chocolate, melted
1 cup chopped nuts

Cream sugar and butter; add well-beaten eggs and mashed potatoes. Combine dry ingredients and add alternately with milk. Stir in melted chocolate and nuts. Bake in a greased tube pan at 350° for about 1 hour.

❦ Irish Potato Cake No. 1

(10-INCH TUBE PAN)

1 cup butter	1 teaspoon ground nutmeg
2 cups sugar	½ cup milk
2 cups cooked mashed potatoes	2 cups all-purpose flour
	1 tablespoon soda
1 teaspoon vanilla extract	½ cup cocoa
1 teaspoon lemon extract	4 eggs, well beaten
1 teaspoon ground cloves	1 cup chopped nuts
1 teaspoon ground allspice	1 cup raisins
1 teaspoon ground cinnamon	¼ cup all-purpose flour

Cream butter and sugar. Add potatoes, extracts, and spices and mix well. Add milk. Combine flour, soda, and cocoa and add to creamed mixture. Add well-beaten eggs. Dredge nuts and raisins with ¼ cup flour and add to batter. Pour into a greased 10-inch tube pan and bake at 300° for 2 hours.

❦ Irish Potato Cake No. 2

(TWO 9-INCH LAYER PANS)

½ cup butter or margarine	2 teaspoons baking powder
2 cups sugar	¼ teaspoon salt
1 teaspoon vanilla extract	1 teaspoon soda
1 teaspoon cocoa	½ cup milk
1 cup warm mashed potatoes	1 cup nuts, chopped fine
2 cups all-purpose flour	3 egg whites, beaten light

Cream butter and sugar. Add vanilla, cocoa, and potatoes. Add sifted dry ingredients alternately with milk. Fold in nuts and beaten egg whites. Bake in two greased 9-inch layer pans at 350° for 35 minutes. Frost with Cooked Cream Frosting.

❦ Prune Cake

(LOAF PAN)

½ cup shortening
1 cup sugar
1 egg, beaten
2¼ cups all-purpose flour
1 teaspoon soda
1 teaspoon ground cinnamon

½ cup sour milk
1¼ cups cooked, pitted prunes
1 teaspoon grated lemon rind
 or vanilla extract or both
¾ cup chopped pecans

Cream shortening and add sugar gradually. Add well-beaten egg and mix well. Combine dry ingredients and add alternately with milk. Add coarsely chopped prunes last with lemon rind and vanilla. Add pecans. Pour into greased and lined loaf pan and bake at 350° about 1 hour.

❦ Prune Layer Cake

(TWO 9-INCH LAYER PANS)

½ cup butter or margarine
1½ cups sugar
3 eggs
2¼ cups sifted cake flour
¾ teaspoon salt
1 teaspoon baking powder
2 teaspoons ground cinnamon

1 teaspoon ground nutmeg
¾ teaspoon ground cloves
¾ teaspoon ground allspice
1 teaspoon soda
1 cup buttermilk
1¼ cups chopped, cooked
 prunes

Cream butter or margarine and sugar until well blended. Add eggs, one at a time, and beat well. Sift dry ingredients and add alternately with the buttermilk. Fold in prunes. Bake in two 9-inch layer cake pans at 350° for 35 to 40 minutes.

❦ Jet Prune Cake

(THREE 9-INCH LAYER PANS)

4 cups sifted cake flour
2 teaspoons soda
3 cups sugar
6 eggs
2 cups vegetable oil
2 cups buttermilk

2 teaspoons ground nutmeg
2 teaspoons ground cinnamon
1 teaspoon salt
2 cups chopped, cooked
    prunes

Sift cake flour, soda, and sugar together. Beat eggs for 1 minute. Add eggs and remaining ingredients to flour mixture and beat 3 minutes. Pour into three greased and floured 9-inch pans. Bake in 350° oven for 35 to 40 minutes. Frost with a white frosting.

❦ Pumpkin Cake

(LOAF PAN)

2 cups all-purpose flour
½ teaspoon salt
½ teaspoon soda
3 teaspoons baking powder
½ cup shortening
½ cup white sugar
1 cup brown sugar

2 eggs
2 tablespoons dark corn syrup
½ cup buttermilk
¾ cup cooked, strained
    pumpkin
⅔ cup chopped nuts
1 teaspoon vanilla extract

Mix and sift the flour, salt, soda, and baking powder. Cream the shortening, add the sugars gradually, and cream thoroughly. Add the eggs to creamed mixture one at a time, beating well after each addition. Combine syrup, buttermilk, pumpkin, nuts, and vanilla. Add to the creamed mixture alternately with the flour mixture, stirring after each addition until barely smooth. Grease only the bottom of a loaf pan; line with waxed paper and pour in the batter. Bake at 350° for about 1 hour.

❦ Pumpkin-Raisin-Nut Cake

(TWO 9-INCH LAYER PANS)

2 cups sugar	¾ cup seedless raisins
1 cup cooking oil	1 cup nuts (your choice)
4 eggs	¼ cup cooking oil
2 cups self-rising flour	¼ cup self-rising flour
2 teaspoons ground cinnamon	
½ teaspoon ground nutmeg	
1 (No. 2) can pumpkin or 2	
cups fresh, cooked	
pumpkin	

Using medium speed of electric mixer, cream sugar and cooking oil until smooth. Add eggs, one at a time, mixing thoroughly after each addition. Sift flour with spices three times. Add to creamed mixture and mix until smooth. Add pumpkin and mix thoroughly. Mix the raisins and nuts with the ¼ cup cooking oil and the ¼ cup flour. Using low speed of mixer add mixture to cake batter. Pour into two greased and floured 9-inch layer cake pans (round or square). Bake at 325° for 30 to 35 minutes or until cake is done.

While cake is warm, frost with Lemon-Cheese Frosting or your own favorite frosting.

❦ Pumpkin-Spice Cake

(LOAF PAN)

½ cup butter	1 teaspoon soda
1 cup sugar	½ teaspoon ground allspice or
1 egg	1 teaspoon pumpkin pie
1 cup hot mashed pumpkin	spice
2 cups all-purpose flour	½ teaspoon ground cloves
¼ teaspoon salt	1 cup chopped nuts

Cream butter and sugar. Add egg and blend well. Stir pumpkin into creamed mixture. Mix in dry ingredients, adding nuts at the very last. Pour into a greased loaf pan and bake at 350° for 1 hour to 1 hour and 10 minutes.

🍂 Raisin Cake

(LOAF PAN)

1 cup seedless raisins	1 teaspoon soda
2 cups hot water	1 teaspoon ground cloves
½ cup shortening	1 teaspoon ground cinnamon
1 cup sugar	1 teaspoon ground nutmeg
1⅓ cups all-purpose flour	½ cup finely chopped nuts

Simmer raisins in the water for 10 minutes. Remove from heat; add shortening and stir until melted. Cool. Combine dry ingredients; add nuts and add this mixture to the raisin mixture. Put into a greased loaf pan and bake at 350° for 35 to 40 minutes.

🍂 Raisin-Nut Cake

(TWO 9-INCH LAYER PANS)

½ cup shortening	1 teaspoon salt
1 cup white sugar	1 cup buttermilk
¾ cup brown sugar (packed)	½ cup chopped pecans
3 egg yolks	½ cup dark or light seedless
2 cups plus 2 teaspoons	raisins
all-purpose flour	1 tablespoon maple flavoring
1 teaspoon baking powder	3 egg whites, beaten stiff
¾ teaspoon soda	

Cream shortening and sugars; add egg yolks, one at a time, beating well after each addition. Sift dry ingredients together. Put buttermilk, nuts, and raisins in blender, or chop very fine. Add this mixture alternately with dry ingredients to creamed mixture. Add flavoring; fold in stiffly beaten egg whites. Put batter in two 9-inch layers, three 8-inch layers, or a 13- x 9- x 2-inch pan. Grease pans before adding batter. Bake at 350° about 25 to 35 minutes. When cool, cover with Brown Sugar Frosting.

❦ Raisin-Pecan Cake

(10-INCH TUBE PAN)

1 cup butter	½ teaspoon salt
2 cups sugar	2 pounds seedless raisins
6 eggs, beaten	1 pound (4 cups) chopped
½ cup molasses	pecans
2 teaspoons soda	½ cup flour
3 cups all-purpose flour	

Cream butter and sugar until smooth. Add beaten eggs and mix well. Stir in molasses, to which soda has been added. Combine 3 cups flour and salt and add to creamed mixture. Coat raisins and pecans with ½ cup flour and stir into batter, which will be very stiff. Place batter in a 10-inch tube pan, which has been lined with well-oiled heavy brown paper. Bake at 250° for 4 hours. Cool in pan; then turn out on cake rack and remove brown paper. Wrap in a cloth that has been dampened with grape juice. Store several days before serving.

❦ Raisin-Orange Cake

(13- x 9- x 2-INCH PAN)

2 cups sifted all-purpose flour	1 unpeeled navel orange,
1 teaspoon soda	diced
1 teaspoon salt	1 cup seedless raisins
1 teaspoon baking powder	1 cup sugar
2 eggs	1 cup sour milk or buttermilk
½ cup soft shortening	

Have all ingredients at room temperature. Sift flour, soda, salt, and baking powder together into mixing bowl. Put eggs, shortening, orange, raisins, sugar, and sour milk in glass container of electric blender; cover and blend till orange is well cut, about 30 seconds. Stop blender and stir mixture down at the end of 10 seconds and again at the end of 20 seconds. Pour blended mixture over sifted flour mixture and stir lightly until flour is taken up. Pour into greased 13- x 9- x 2-inch pan. Bake at 350° until browned and done, about 35 to 40 minutes. Cool before frosting. Frost as desired.

❦ Cream Raisin Cake

(TWO 9-INCH LAYER PANS)

½ cup butter
1½ cups brown sugar
2 eggs, beaten
2 cups all-purpose flour
3 teaspoons baking powder
½ teaspoon salt

½ teaspoon ground allspice
½ teaspoon ground cinnamon
½ teaspoon ground nutmeg
1 cup sour milk
1 teaspoon vanilla extract

Cream butter and sugar; add beaten eggs. Add dry ingredients alternately with milk. Add vanilla. Bake in two 9-inch, greased and paper-lined pans at 350° about 30 minutes. Use Raisin Cream Filling between layers and on top and sides of cake.

❦ Raisin-Date-Pecan Cake

(10-INCH TUBE PAN)

1 cup butter
2 cups sugar
4 eggs
1⅓ cups buttermilk
1 teaspoon soda
4 cups all-purpose flour,
   divided

1 cup seedless raisins
1 cup finely chopped pecans
1 (1-pound) box pitted dates,
   chopped
4 tablespoons grated orange
   peel

Cream butter and sugar until light and fluffy. Add eggs, one at a time, beating well after each addition. Add buttermilk and mixture of soda and 3 cups flour and mix well. Mix 1 cup flour with raisins, pecans, and dates. Stir until all pieces are coated; then add to creamed mixture. Add orange peel and mix well. Put batter in a greased 10-inch tube pan and bake at 350° about 1½ hours.

❧ Shortcake

(COOKIE SHEET)

2 cups all-purpose flour	⅔ to ¾ cup milk
4 tablespoons baking powder	Margarine for hot shortcake
2 tablespoons sugar	Sliced, sweetened
½ teaspoon salt	strawberries or other fruit
6 tablespoons margarine	Whipped cream

Combine flour, baking powder, sugar, and salt in a bowl. Blend in margarine, using a pastry blender or two knives, until mixture resembles coarse meal. Add the milk and mix together thoroughly. Knead very lightly for a few seconds on a floured board. Pat to about ½ inch thickness. Cut with a very large cookie cutter. Place on lightly greased cookie sheet and bake at 450° for about 10 to 12 minutes, or until nicely browned. Spread the layers with margarine. Put together with sweetened fruit. Top with more fruit and whipped cream.

❧ Strawberry Shortcake No. 1

(TWO 8-INCH LAYER PANS)

2 cups all-purpose flour	⅔ cup milk
3 teaspoons baking powder	Melted butter
½ teaspoon salt	1 quart fresh strawberries
2 tablespoons sugar	1½ cups sugar
⅓ cup shortening	Whipped cream

Sift flour, baking powder, salt, and 2 tablespoons sugar. Add shortening and cut in until mixture resembles coarse crumbs. Add milk and mix well. Divide dough and pat into two round 8-inch cake pans. Brush with melted butter and bake at 450° for 15 to 18 minutes.

Prepare strawberries and mix with 1½ cups sugar. Reserve some whole berries for garnish and crush the other berries with a fork. Let sit until sugar is melted and syrup forms. Spread berries between layers of shortcake and on top. Serve with whipped cream, garnished with whole berries.

Strawberry Shortcake

(COOKIE SHEET)

2 cups all-purpose flour
3 teaspoons baking powder
¾ teaspoon salt
3 tablespoons sugar
1 (3-ounce) package cream cheese, softened
3 tablespoons softened butter or margarine
1 egg, beaten
About ½ cup milk
Melted butter
Sweetened strawberries
Whipped cream

Sift together flour, baking powder, salt, and sugar. Cut in cream cheese and butter. Pour beaten egg into measuring cup and add enough milk to measure ¾ cup. Gradually stir into the flour mixture. Knead dough about 20 seconds. Divide dough into two parts; roll each part ½ inch thick. Cut six circles from each half of dough. Spread one circle with melted butter and place another circle on top. Bake at 425° about 15 minutes.

When done, separate layers. Spread each layer with butter. Put sweetened berries on one circle and top with other circle. Add strawberries and top with whipped cream. Continue until all circles have been used. Yield: 6 servings.

Mississippi Strawberry Shortcake

(13- x 9-INCH PAN)

2 cups commercial biscuit mix
2 tablespoons sugar
½ cup milk
4 cups sweetened strawberries
1 cup whipped cream

Combine biscuit mix and sugar in mixing bowl; add milk and stir until well mixed. Turn out on floured board and knead lightly. Roll out about ¼ inch thick and cut into 3- or 4-inch circles or pat dough in 13- x 9-inch pan. Bake at 450° for about 8 minutes.

Split rounds or cut squares, fill with sweetened strawberries, and spoon a few berries on top. Cover with whipped cream. Serve immediately. Yield: 6 to 8 servings.

❦ Fresh Strawberry Cake

(THREE 8-INCH LAYER PANS)

1 stick butter
⅓ cup shortening
1¾ cups sugar
½ cup sliced fresh strawberries
    or drained chopped frozen
    strawberries
1 (6-ounce) package
    strawberry-flavored gelatin

2⅔ cups all-purpose flour
3½ teaspoons baking powder
½ teaspoon salt
1⅓ cups milk
1 teaspoon vanilla extract
4 egg whites

Cream butter, shortening, and sugar until fluffy. Add strawberries and gelatin; beat well.

Sift together dry ingredients and add alternately with milk. Add vanilla; beat well. Fold in egg whites. Turn into three lightly greased and floured 8-inch cake pans. Bake at 350° for 30 to 35 minutes. Frost with Strawberry Frosting.

❦ Easy Strawberry Cake

(THREE 8- OR 9-INCH LAYER PANS)

1 package white cake mix
1 tablespoon all-purpose flour
¾ cup salad oil
½ cup water
½ cup frozen strawberries,
    thawed to a mush

1 (3-ounce) package
    strawberry-flavored gelatin
4 eggs

Combine all ingredients except eggs in a large mixing bowl. Add eggs, one at a time, beating after each addition. Bake in three greased 8- or 9-inch layer cake pans at 350° for 25 to 30 minutes. Frost as desired.

❦ Strawberry Refrigerator Cake

(SPRINGFORM PAN)

6 ladyfingers or 1 small sponge cake	⅓ cup heavy cream
3 tablespoons sugar	¼ teaspoon vanilla extract
1¼ cups crushed strawberries	1 tablespoon chopped nuts

Line springform pan with split ladyfingers or sliced sponge cake. Add sugar to strawberries. Whip cream with vanilla. Cover cake with berries, then a layer of whipped cream. Repeat in layers until all material is used, saving part of cream for top of cake. Sprinkle with nuts and chill for 8 hours.

❦ Black Forest Torte

(FOUR 9-INCH LAYER PANS)

1¾ cups all-purpose flour	1¼ cups water
1¾ cups sugar	1 teaspoon vanilla extract
1¼ teaspoons soda	3 eggs
1 teaspoon salt	Chocolate Filling
¼ teaspoon baking powder	Cream Filling
⅔ cup soft margarine or butter	½ of 4-ounce sweet chocolate bar
4 (1-ounce) squares unsweetened chocolate, melted and cooled	

Measure into a large mixing bowl: flour, sugar, soda, salt, baking powder, margarine, melted chocolate, water, and vanilla. Beat at low speed to blend. Then beat at medium speed for 2 minutes, scraping sides and bottom of bowl frequently. Then add eggs and beat for an additional 2 minutes.

Spoon into four 9-inch round layer cake pans which have been greased (approximately 1¼ cups batter in each). Layers will be very thin. If preferred, only two layers may be baked at a time. Bake at 350° from 15 to 18 minutes or until wooden pick inserted in center comes out clean. Cool slightly; then remove from pans. Cool thoroughly before adding filling.

Place bottom layer of cake on serving plate and spread with half of Chocolate Filling. Add another layer and spread with half of Cream

Filling. Repeat layers, having Cream Filling on top. Using a vegetable peeler, make chocolate curls with the ½ bar of sweet chocolate. Decorate top completely. Sides of torte do not have frosting. Wrap with plastic wrap and refrigerate until ready to serve. Yield: 12 servings.

Chocolate Filling

Melt 1½ sweet chocolate bars (4 ounces each) over hot water. Cool; blend in ¾ cup margarine. Stir in ½ cup chopped almonds or pecans.

Cream Filling

Whip together 2 cups whipping cream with 1 tablespoon sugar and 1 teaspoon vanilla; do not overbeat.

❦ Torte Cake

(TWO 8-INCH LAYER PANS)

½ cup shortening	¼ teaspoon salt
½ cup sugar	½ teaspoon vanilla extract
4 egg yolks	4 egg whites
5 tablespoons milk	1 cup powdered sugar
1 cup cake flour	½ cup chopped nuts
1 teaspoon baking powder	

Cream shortening and sugar. Add beaten yolks. Stir in milk. Beat in sifted flour, baking powder, and salt; add vanilla. Put in two 8-inch layer cake pans which have been greased slightly. Beat egg whites until stiff. Add powdered sugar. Beat well and spread on top of each layer. Sprinkle with chopped nuts. Bake at 350° until browned.

Filling

Juice and rind of 1 lemon	1 tablespoon cornstarch
1 cup sugar	1 egg, beaten

Combine lemon juice, rind, sugar, cornstarch, and egg and cook in top of double boiler until thick. Spread between cooled cake layers.

❦ Butterscotch-Nut Torte

(SPRINGFORM OR TORTE PAN)

6 egg yolks	6 egg whites, beaten stiff
1½ cups sugar	2 cups graham cracker
1 teaspoon baking powder	crumbs
2 teaspoons vanilla extract	1 cup chopped pecans
1 teaspoon almond extract	½ pint whipping cream

Beat egg yolks well. Add sugar and baking powder. Add flavorings. Mix well. Beat egg whites until stiff but not dry. Fold in egg yolk mixture, cracker crumbs, and nuts. Pour into lightly greased springform pan and bake at 325° for 35 to 40 minutes. Cool and frost with whipped cream. When ready to serve, spoon Butterscotch Sauce over each serving.

Butterscotch Sauce

1 cup brown sugar	¼ cup water
1 tablespoon all-purpose flour	2 eggs
¼ cup butter	½ teaspoon vanilla extract
¼ cup orange juice	

Combine sugar and flour. Add remaining ingredients in order given, except vanilla. Cook in top part of double boiler until thick. Add vanilla and cool.

Cut torte and pour sauce over individual pieces before serving.

❦ French Pecan Torte

(12-INCH SPRINGFORM PAN)

1 heaping tablespoon	1 cup sugar
breadcrumbs	8 egg yolks, beaten
4 cups finely ground pecans	Juice of ½ lemon
1 grated lemon rind	2 cups cream
8 egg whites	Pecan halves, garnish

Combine breadcrumbs, ground pecans, and lemon rind in a large mixing bowl. Place the 8 egg whites in another mixing bowl and beat until stiff, gradually adding the sugar.

In still another installment beat the already beaten egg yolks with lemon juice until thick and lemon colored.

Now pour the egg whites over the pecan mixture. Then very carefully fold ingredients together, now pouring the egg yolk mixture over and into the egg whites. *Do not stir mixture or cake will fall!* Careful folding of ingredients is absolutely essential.

When properly folded together, pour the whole mixture into a greased 12-inch springform pan and bake at 375° for 45 minutes. Remove from oven and cool in the pan. Remove cooled cake from pan and slice in half, side to side, making two layers.

Whip the heavy cream until thick. Spread bottom half with whipped cream, and replace top layer.

Frost the top and sides of cake with remaining whipped cream. Garnish artistically with pecan halves.

Party Torte

(TWO 9-INCH LAYER PANS)

1 teaspoon vanilla extract	8 egg whites
1 teaspoon vinegar	2 cups sugar

Add vanilla and vinegar to the egg whites and beat until the mixture forms peaks. Add the sugar gradually, about a tablespoon at a time, beating all the time. Have ready two 9-inch layer cake pans, lightly greased on the bottoms and lined with brown paper, then grease paper. Bake at 300° for 1¼ hours. Remove from oven and let set a few minutes. Turn onto cake rack and cool completely before putting Filling between layers.

Filling

2 cups whipping cream	¾ cup chopped drained
1 cup or small can crushed	maraschino cherries
pineapple, well drained	1 cup chopped pecans

Whip cream until stiff and fold in pineapple, cherries, and pecans. Put a layer of the cream mixture between the two torte layers and then ice the top and sides. Store in refrigerator 12 hours or more before serving. Cut as you would a cake.

❦ Meringue Nut Torte—Custard Filling

(TWO 9-INCH LAYER PANS)

Batter

½ cup butter or margarine
½ cup sugar
3 egg yolks, beaten
1½ cups all-purpose flour

1½ teaspoons baking powder
¼ teaspoon salt
½ cup milk
½ teaspoon vanilla extract

Topping

5 egg whites
1 cup sugar

Coconut

Cream butter and sugar together until smooth. Add beaten egg yolks. Combine flour, baking powder, and salt, and add to creamed mixture alternately with milk and vanilla combined. Pour batter into two greased and floured 9-inch cake pans. Cover with Topping.

For the topping, beat egg whites until stiff; gradually add sugar and continue beating until egg whites stand in peaks. Spread topping over two cake layers; sprinkle tops with coconut. Bake at 375° for 20 minutes, or until cake tests done. Let layers cool in pans. Then loosen around edges with knife. Place cakes on racks. Coconut which falls off may be sprinkled on layers again. Spread bottom layer with custard, sprinkle with nuts, and add second layer. Spread top layer with custard and cover with nuts. Store cake in refrigerator.

Custard Filling

6 tablespoons sugar
6 tablespoons cornstarch
1½ cups milk

2 egg yolks, beaten
1 teaspoon vanilla extract
1 cup chopped nuts

Combine sugar and cornstarch in saucepan. Gradually add milk and stir until smooth. Cook, over low heat, stirring constantly, until milk almost reaches boiling point. Pour small amount over beaten egg yolks. Return to saucepan and cook until thick. Add vanilla and chill. Sprinkle nuts over cake.

☙ Huguenot Torte

(TWO 11- X 8-INCH PANS)

4 eggs
3 cups sugar
8 tablespoons all-purpose
  flour

5 teaspoons baking powder
2 cups chopped tart apples
2 cups chopped pecans

Beat whole eggs until very frothy and lemon colored. Add other ingredients and mix well; pour into two 11- x 8-inch well-buttered pans. Bake at 350° about 45 minutes or until crusty and brown. Let cool. Cut in squares; lift with pancake turner, keeping crusty part on top. Serve with whipped cream.

☙ Upside-Down Pecan Cake

(8-OR 9-INCH PAN)

4 tablespoons butter or
  margarine
1 cup brown sugar, firmly
  packed

1 tablespoon hot water
1 cup pecans, coarsely
  chopped

Melt butter in bottom of 8- or 9-inch cake pan. Put in brown sugar and water and keep over low heat until well mixed. Pour pecans on top and set mixture aside until cake is mixed.

Cake Mixture

2 egg yolks
1 cup sugar
1 teaspoon vanilla extract
1 cup all-purpose flour

1½ teaspoons baking powder
½ teaspoon salt
¾ cup hot water
2 egg whites, beaten

Beat egg yolks; add sugar and vanilla, and beat well. Add sifted dry ingredients alternately with hot water. Fold in stiffly beaten egg whites. Pour over nut mixture and bake at 325° about 30 minutes Turn out of pan while still hot.

❧ Upside-Down Cake

(LARGE SKILLET)

½ cup butter or margarine	1 teaspoon vanilla extract
1 cup brown sugar	1 cup all-purpose flour
1 (No. 2) can sliced pineapple	½ teaspoon salt
6 or 8 cherries	1 teaspoon baking powder
2 tablespoons pecan halves	½ cup boiling milk
2 eggs	1 tablespoon butter or
1 cup sugar	margarine

Melt butter in large skillet. Add brown sugar and mix. Place pineapple slices on mixture. Put cherry in center of each slice and sprinkle pecans over mixture. Beat the eggs; add sugar gradually and stir in vanilla. Sift flour, salt, and baking powder and add them next, still beating. Scald milk and add the butter, allowing to melt in the milk. Add this last and give a dozen more beats. Pour batter over pineapple slices. Bake at 350° for 30 to 35 minutes.

Note: Other fruits may be used: dried cooked apricots or peaches, or drained canned peaches.

This cake may dry out quickly, but may be topped with whipped cream to moisten.

❧ Pineapple Upside-Down Cake

(SKILLET OR HEAVY BAKING PAN)

½ cup butter or margarine	1 teaspoon baking powder
1 cup brown sugar	⅛ teaspoon salt
1 (No. 2) can sliced pineapple	1 cup sugar
Maraschino cherries	3 egg yolks, beaten
About 12 pecan halves	5 tablespoons pineapple juice
1 cup cake flour	3 egg whites, beaten

Melt butter in large baking pan. Spread brown sugar evenly in pan and arrange pineapple slices on sugar. Put cherries in centers of slices and fill in spaces with pecan halves. Sift dry ingredients. Add egg yolks and pineapple juice. Fold in stiffly beaten egg whites. Pour batter over pineapple. Bake at 375° for 30 to 35 minutes. Turn upside down on cake plate.

Chocolate Upside-Down Cake

(8-INCH SQUARE LAYER PAN)

½ cup chopped nuts	1½ teaspoons baking powder
1 (6-ounce) package semi-sweet chocolate pieces	½ teaspoon salt
	¾ cup sugar
1 cup sifted powdered milk	¼ cup soft shortening
⅓ cup evaporated milk	1 egg
1 cup plus 2 tablespoons all-purpose flour	½ cup milk
	1 teaspoon vanilla extract

Sprinkle nuts into waxed paper-lined 8-inch square pan. Melt chocolate pieces over hot (not boiling) water. Remove from heat. Add powdered sugar and milk and beat well. Spread over nuts.

Sift flour together with baking powder and salt and set aside. Cream sugar and shortening. Beat in egg. Add flour mixture to creamed mixture alternately with milk and vanilla.

Pour over chocolate mixture in pan. Bake at 350° for 45 to 50 minutes. Let stand in pan 5 minutes. Invert on rack. Remove waxed paper. Cool. To serve, cut in 2-inch squares.

Cake Mix Upside-Down Cake

(13- x 9- x 2-INCH PAN)

1 (No. 2) can fruit pie filling	2 sticks margarine, melted
1 box white cake mix	

Put pie filling in bottom of 13- x 9- x 2-inch pan. Mix cake as directed on package and pour over fruit. Pour melted margarine over top. Bake at 350° about 30 to 35 minutes.

❦ White Moon Cake

(THREE 9-INCH LAYER PANS)

3 cups all-purpose flour	2 cups sugar
3 teaspoons baking powder	1 cup milk
½ teaspoon salt	1 teaspoon vanilla extract
⅔ cup butter or shortening	5 egg whites, stiffly beaten

Combine flour, baking powder, and salt, and set aside. Cream butter or shortening, add sugar, and cream until well blended. Add flour alternately with the milk. Add vanilla, and fold in stiffly beaten egg whites. Pour into three greased 9-inch layer cake pans. Bake at 325° for 15 minutes, then increase to 350° and bake for about 15 minutes longer. Frost as desired.

❦ White Layer Cake No. 1

(TWO 8-INCH LAYER PANS)

2 cups cake flour	1½ teaspoons lemon juice
1 teaspoon baking powder	6 egg whites, beaten stiff
¼ teaspoon salt	1¼ cups powdered sugar
¾ cup butter or margarine	

Sift together cake flour, baking powder, and salt; work butter or margarine until creamy. Add dry ingredients and beat until smooth. Beat in lemon juice. Beat egg whites until stiff; fold in powdered sugar gradually. Fold egg white mixture into creamed mixture. Put into two greased 8-inch layer cake pans. Bake at 375° for 25 minutes. Frost as desired.

❦ White Layer Cake No. 2

(TWO 8-INCH LAYER PANS)

½ cup butter	¼ teaspoon salt
1½ cups sugar	1 cup ice water
2½ cups all-purpose flour	2 teaspoons vanilla extract
3 teaspoons baking powder	4 egg whites, beaten

Cream butter (do not use margarine) and sugar until fluffy. Sift dry ingredients together. Add to creamed mixture alternately with ice water, beginning and ending with flour mixture. Add vanilla. Fold in stiffly beaten egg whites. Put batter in two greased 8-inch layer pans. Bake at 350° for 25 to 30 minutes.

❦ Buttermilk White Layer Cake No. 1

(TWO 8- OR 9-INCH LAYER PANS)

¾ cup vegetable shortening
1½ cups sugar
1 teaspoon vanilla extract
3 cups all-purpose flour
3 teaspoons baking powder

½ teaspoon soda
1 teaspoon salt
1¼ cups buttermilk
¾ cup egg whites (about 6 eggs)

Cream shortening. Gradually add sugar. Add vanilla. Combine dry ingredients. Add dry ingredients and buttermilk alternately to sugar and shortening mixture. Fold in egg whites which have been whipped to frothy stage. Bake in two greased 8- or 9-inch cake pans at 350° for about 30 minutes, or until cake begins to leave corners of pans. Frost as desired.

❦ Buttermilk White Layer Cake No. 2

(THREE 8-INCH LAYER PANS)

¾ cup vegetable shortening
2¼ cups sugar
8 egg whites
3 cups all-purpose flour
¼ teaspoon salt

¾ teaspoon cream of tartar
¾ cup buttermilk
1 teaspoon vanilla extract
⅜ teaspoon soda
2 tablespoons warm water

Cream shortening and sugar. Add unbeaten egg whites alternately with flour, salt, and cream of tartar which have been sifted together. Add all of buttermilk at one time before adding last portion of dry ingredients. Stir in vanilla and beat well. Dissolve soda in warm water and add last; stir well. Bake in three oiled 8-inch layer cake pans at 350° from 20 to 25 minutes or until cake pulls away from sides of pan. This cake can also be baked in a large tube pan about 1 hour, or a 13- x 9-inch pan about 40 to 45 minutes. Frost, if desired.

❦ White Sheet Cake
(13- x 9-INCH PAN)

1 cup butter	1 cup milk
2 cups sugar, sifted	1 teaspoon vanilla extract
3½ cups cake flour	¼ teaspoon almond extract
½ teaspoon salt	7 or 8 egg whites
4 teaspoons baking powder	⅛ teaspoon salt

Cream butter until soft. Sift in sugar gradually. Blend these ingredients until they are very light and creamy. Sift cake flour before measuring. After measuring, resift it twice with the ½ teaspoon salt and baking powder. Add flour in three parts alternately with milk divided into three parts. Beat the batter until it is smooth after each addition. Add vanilla and almond extract. Whip egg whites until stiff but not dry. Add ⅛ teaspoon salt. Fold egg whites lightly into cake batter. Bake in a greased 13- x 9-inch pan at 350° about 40 minutes, or in three 8-inch pans for 25 minutes at 375°.

❦ Apricot Cake
(TWO 8-INCH LAYER PANS)

½ cup shortening	1¾ cups cake flour
1 cup sugar	½ teaspoon salt
2 eggs, well beaten	2½ teaspoons baking powder
1 teaspoon vanilla extract	½ cup milk

Cream shortening and sugar together until smooth. Add beaten eggs and beat until light. Add vanilla. Sift together flour, salt, and baking powder. Add to creamed mixture alternately with milk. Begin and end with dry ingredients. Beat well. Put batter in two 8-inch layer cake pans greased and lined with waxed paper and greased again. Bake at 375° for 25 to 30 minutes. Let stand 5 minutes, then turn out on racks to cool.

Apricot Filling and Meringue

2 cups dried apricots	1 teaspoon grated lemon rind
2 cups water	2 egg whites
1 cup sugar	2 tablespoons sugar
¼ teaspoon salt	1 teaspoon lemon juice

Wash apricots; add 2 cups water and simmer in a covered saucepan until tender (about 30 minutes). Put through a sieve or colander and add 1 cup sugar, ¼ teaspoon salt, and 1 teaspoon grated lemon rind. Cook slowly until thick, stirring constantly.

Split cake layers crosswise. Save ⅔ cup of apricot mixture for the meringue and spread the rest between the cake layers. Beat the 2 egg whites until foamy. Gradually add 2 tablespoons sugar and beat well. Fold in remaining ⅔ cup apricot puree and 1 teaspoon lemon juice. Frost top and sides of the cake with apricot meringue.

❦ Broken Glass Cake
(13- x 9- x 2-inch pan)

3 (3-ounce) packages fruit-flavored gelatin (assorted)	½ cup hot fruit juice
	2 (2-ounce) packages whipped topping
2 cups vanilla wafer or graham cracker crumbs	1 teaspoon vanilla extract
½ cup sugar	¼ cup sugar
1 stick margarine, melted	1 cup milk
1 envelope unflavored gelatin	Chopped nuts, if desired
2 tablespoons cold water	

Prepare the three fruit gelatins according to package directions (select assorted colors and flavors). Pour into three shallow pans and keep in refrigerator overnight. Mix 1¾ cups of the crumbs with ½ cup sugar and melted margarine; use to line bottom and sides of a 13- x 9- x 2-inch pan. Dissolve unflavored gelatin in cold water; let stand 5 minutes. Add hot juice and heat until gelatin is dissolved; cool. Whip packaged topping with vanilla, ¼ cup sugar, and 1 cup milk. Fold unflavored gelatin mixture into this mixture.

Cut fruit gelatin into small cubes and fold into topping mixture. This dessert gives the appearance of colored glass cubes. Pour into crumb-lined pan and sprinkle with remainder of crumbs and nuts. Chill and serve. Yield: 12 to 16 servings.

❦ Blackberry Cake

(THREE 8- OR 9-INCH LAYER PANS)

1 cup butter or margarine
2 cups sugar
4 eggs, beaten
2¾ cups all-purpose flour
3 tablespoons cocoa
4 teaspoons soda

1 teaspoon ground cloves
1 teaspoon ground allspice
1 teaspoon ground cinnamon
2 cups canned blackberries
    and juice
1 teaspoon vanilla extract

Cream butter or margarine; add sugar and beaten eggs and mix well. Sift dry ingredients. Add to creamed mixture alternately with berries. Add vanilla. Bake in three 8- or 9-inch greased layer pans at 350° for 20 to 25 minutes. Put layers together with your favorite white or caramel frosting.

❦ Butter Sponge Cake

(TWO 9-INCH LAYER PANS)

11 egg yolks
2 cups sifted sugar
1 cup scalded milk
1 teaspoon vanilla extract

2¼ cups sifted cake flour
2 teaspoons baking powder
½ cup melted butter or
    margarine

Beat egg yolks and sugar until light colored and very fluffy. Add scalded milk and vanilla, beating constantly. Add flour and baking powder sifted together. Fold in melted butter or margarine. Batter will be very thin. Pour into two 9-inch, well-greased, layer cake pans. Bake at 350° for 30 to 40 minutes. Invert pans and cool before removing.

❦ Pudding Mix Cake

(13- x 9- x 2-INCH PAN)

1 box yellow cake mix
1 (4½-ounce) package
    pudding mix

4 eggs
½ cup water
½ cup salad oil

Combine cake and pudding mixes in large electric mixer bowl; add eggs, water, and salad oil. Beat 4 minutes at medium speed on electric mixer; scrape bowl often. Pour into greased, waxed-paper lined, 13- x 9- x 2-inch cake pan. Bake at 350° about 45 minutes. Frost as desired.

❦ Bishop's Cake
(LOAF PAN)

3 eggs, well beaten	1 (6-ounce) package
1 teaspoon vanilla extract	semi-sweet chocolate
1 cup sugar	pieces
1½ cups all-purpose flour	1 cup chopped dates
1½ teaspoons baking powder	1 cup halved candied cherries
¼ teaspoon salt	2 cups chopped nuts

Combine eggs, vanilla, and sugar and beat well. Combine dry ingredients and add to chocolate pieces, fruit, and nuts. Fold this mixture into egg mixture. Mixture will be very stiff. Pack into loaf pan which has been greased and lined with double thickness of greased paper. Bake at 325° for 1½ hours.

❦ Buttermilk Cake
(TUBE PAN)

2 cups sifted cake flour	1 teaspoon soda
1 cup raisins	1 cup salad oil
1 cup chopped nuts	1 cup buttermilk
1 teaspoon ground cinnamon	3 eggs
1 teaspoon ground allspice	1½ cups sugar

Sift a little flour over raisins and nuts. Combine rest of flour with other dry ingredients in mixing bowl. Add salad oil, buttermilk, eggs, and sugar; beat until smooth. Stir in nuts and raisins. Pour into floured and greased tube pan. Bake at 350° for 1 hour.

Topping

Combine ¾ cup buttermilk, ¾ cup sugar, 2 tablespoons light corn syrup, 1 teaspoon soda, 1 teaspoon vanilla extract, and ⅓ stick butter. Heat until bubbly. Pour over hot cake right from the oven and do not remove from pan until cool.

❦ Happy Day Cake

(TWO 9-INCH LAYER PANS)

½ cup vegetable shortening	½ teaspoon salt
1½ cups sugar	3 teaspoons baking powder
2 large eggs	1 cup milk
2¼ cups all-purpose flour	1 teaspoon vanilla extract

Cream shortening and sugar. Add eggs and beat until smooth. Add dry ingredients alternately with milk. Add vanilla. Put batter in two greased and floured 9-inch layer cake pans. Bake at 350° for 25 to 30 minutes. Cool and frost as desired.

❦ Yellow Mold Cake

(10-INCH TUBE PAN)

3 sticks butter	2½ cups all-purpose flour
1 (1-pound) box powdered sugar	½ teaspoon salt
	1 teaspoon vanilla extract
6 eggs	1 teaspoon lemon extract

Cream butter and sugar until smooth. Add eggs, one at a time, beating well after each addition. Add flour, salt, vanilla and lemon extracts, and beat well. Bake in greased 10-inch tube pan at 325° for 1 hour.

❦ Cake-Mix Sheet Cake

(13- x 9- x 2-INCH PAN)

1 box white cake mix	2 sticks margarine, melted
1 (No. 2) can fruit, drained (apples, cherries)	

Prepare cake mix according to package directions. Grease 13- x 9- x 2-inch pan and pour drained canned fruit in bottom. Cover with cake batter. Pour melted margarine over cake. Bake as directed on package. Let cool in pan before turning out, or serve in squares from pan.

❦ Gumdrop Cake

(TUBE PAN)

1 cup butter or margarine
2 cups sugar
3 eggs
1 cup applesauce
1 teaspoon vanilla extract
4½ cups all-purpose flour

1 tablespoon baking powder
¼ teaspoon salt
1 pound dates, chopped
1 pound small, spiced
  gumdrops
1 cup chopped pecans

Cream butter; add sugar and cream until smooth. Add eggs and beat well. Combine applesauce and vanilla. Combine all dry ingredients. Mix dates, gumdrops, and nuts in a large bowl and add enough of flour mixture to coat. Add flour mixture to creamed mixture alternately with applesauce. Pour batter over gumdrop mixture and stir just enough to mix well. Put into a greased tube pan lined with heavy brown paper which has been greased. Bake at 300° for about 2 hours.

❦ Cider Cake

(9-INCH SPRINGFORM PAN)

¼ pound butter
¾ cup sugar
2 eggs
2¼ cups cake flour
¼ teaspoon salt
1 teaspoon baking powder

½ teaspoon ground ginger
½ teaspoon ground cinnamon
2 tablespoons grated orange
  rind
¾ cup raisins
⅓ cup cider

Cream the butter; gradually add sugar and beat until fluffy. Add one egg at a time, beating well after each addition. Combine the dry ingredients; add to this mixture the orange rind and raisins. Add to the butter mixture alternately with the cider. Pour batter into greased and floured 9-inch springform or layer cake pan. Bake at 350° for 40 minutes, or until cake tests done.

❧ Harvest Delight Cake

(13- x 9- x 2-inch pan)

2¾ cups all-purpose flour	½ teaspoon ground allspice
2 cups sugar	½ cup soft shortening
1½ teaspoons soda	2 eggs
1½ teaspoons salt	2 cups unsweetened
¼ teaspoon baking powder	applesauce
1 teaspoon ground cinnamon	½ cup chopped pecans
½ teaspoon ground cloves	¼ pound marshmallows

Sift dry ingredients together. Add shortening, eggs, and applesauce; beat until smooth and well blended. Stir in pecans. Pour into greased and floured 13- x 9- x 2-inch pan.

Press whole marshmallows into batter to bottom of pan in four rows, five to each row. Bake at 350° for 50 minutes.

❧ Cola Cake

(TUBE PAN)

2 cups all-purpose flour	3 tablespoons cocoa
2 cups sugar	1 cup cola drink
1½ cups chopped	½ cup buttermilk
marshmallows	1 teaspoon soda
½ cup shortening	2 eggs, beaten
½ cup margarine	

Sift together flour and sugar and stir in marshmallows; set aside. In a saucepan, put the shortening, margarine, cocoa, and cola. Bring to a boil and heat just until shortening and margarine melt. Remove from heat and pour over flour mixture. Stir in buttermilk, soda, and eggs.

Pour into a greased tube pan and bake at 350° for 45 minutes, or until cake tests done. Remove from oven and cool in pan. Cake may crumble slightly. Cake may be baked in a 9- x 9- x 2-inch pan or a loaf pan, but it will take slightly longer to bake. Cover with Cola Frosting.

Note: You do not beat the mixture.

❧ Caramel-Nut Ring

(RING MOLD)

2 tablespoons melted butter or
   margarine
2 tablespoons water
½ cup brown sugar

¼ cup sliced filberts or other
   nuts'
10 or 12 brown-and-serve
   dinner rolls

Combine butter, water, brown sugar, and filberts. Spread this mixture on bottom and sides of a 5-cup ring mold. Press rolls, close together with tops down, over sugar mixture in mold. Bake at 400° for 15 minutes. Let rolls stand in pan 1 minute or longer after removing from oven. Invert mold and remove rolls in one complete ring. Caramel-nut mixture will be on top. Serve immediately. Yield: 5 or 6 servings.

❧ Easter Dawn Cake

(THREE 8- OR 9-INCH LAYER PANS)

⅔ cup soft butter
1¾ cups sugar
2 eggs
1½ teaspoons vanilla extract
3 cups sifted cake flour
2½ teaspoons baking powder
1 teaspoon salt

1¼ cups milk
Red food coloring
¼ teaspoon peppermint
   flavoring, if desired
1 (6½-ounce) package fluffy
   white frosting mix

Beat butter, sugar, eggs, and vanilla 5 minutes at high speed on mixer or by hand until fluffy. Sift dry ingredients together. Add to creamed mixture, 4 tablespoons at a time, alternately with milk (start and end with dry ingredients). Blend on low speed just until smooth. Put two-thirds of the batter into three greased and floured 8- or 9-inch round or square layer pans. To rest of batter add food coloring and peppermint flavoring. Pour here and there over plain batter in pans. Cut through batter with knife several times for marbled effect. Bake at 350° for 30 to 35 minutes or until toothpick inserted in center of cake comes out clean. Frost with fluffy white frosting mix, lightly tinted with red food coloring. For lots of frosting, use 2 packages frosting.

❧ Sad Cake

(13- x 9- x 2-inch pan)

3 eggs	2 cups commercial biscuit mix
1 pound brown sugar	1 cup chopped pecans

Slightly beat three eggs in large bowl. Add brown sugar. Mix well, breaking up all lumps. Add the biscuit mix and pecans, and mix until well moistened. Pour into greased 13- x 9- x 2-inch pan or iron skillet. Bake at 350° for 25 to 30 minutes. This cake falls in the center.

❧ Bohemian Cake

(10-inch tube pan)

¾ cup butter	1 teaspoon vanilla extract
1½ cups sugar	¼ teaspoon lemon extract
4 egg yolks, beaten thoroughly	4 egg whites, beaten stiff
2 cups sifted cake flour	½ teaspoon cream of tartar
½ teaspoon soda	Pecan halves
½ cup milk	

Cream butter and sugar until light and fluffy. Add beaten egg yolks. Add sifted dry ingredients alternately with milk. Add extracts. Fold in egg whites beaten with cream of tartar. Grease and dust a 10-inch tube pan with flour. Line bottom with pecan halves. Pour in batter. Bake at 350° for 45 minutes. When done, turn out so pecans will be on top.

❧ Pinto Fiesta Cake

(10-inch tube pan)

1 cup sugar	½ teaspoon salt
¼ cup butter	1 teaspoon ground cinnamon
1 egg, beaten	½ teaspoon ground cloves
2 cups cooked pinto beans, mashed	½ teaspoon ground allspice
1 cup all-purpose flour	2 cups diced raw apples
1 teaspoon soda	1 cup raisins
	½ cup chopped nuts
	1 teaspoon vanilla extract

Cream sugar and butter, add beaten egg. Add mashed beans. Sift all dry ingredients together and add to sugar mixture. Add apples, raisins, chopped nuts, and vanilla. Pour into well-greased 10-inch tube pan and bake at 375° for 45 minutes. Glaze and decorate with maraschino cherry halves and walnut halves, if desired.

❦ Burnt Sugar Cake
(TWO 9-INCH LAYER PANS)

½ cup sugar	¾ cup butter or shortening
⅓ cup hot water	1¼ cups sugar
3 cups sifted cake flour	3 eggs, unbeaten
3 teaspoons baking powder	1 teaspoon vanilla extract
½ teaspoon salt	⅔ cup milk

Place ½ cup sugar in heavy skillet. Heat, stirring constantly, until sugar is dark brown. Remove from heat, add hot water very slowly, and stir until dissolved. Cool syrup.

Sift dry ingredients together. Cream butter, add 1¼ cups sugar gradually, and cream until light and fluffy. Add eggs, one at a time, beating thoroughly after each addition. Add vanilla and 5 tablespoons of syrup; blend. Add dry ingredients and milk alternately, beating until smooth. Add remainder of syrup. Pour batter in two greased 9-inch layer cake pans. Bake at 350° for 25 to 30 minutes.

❦ Hickory Nut Cake
(TWO 8-INCH LAYER PANS)

½ cup butter or margarine	2 cups sifted cake flour
1¼ cups sugar	3 teaspoons baking powder
2 eggs, separated	¼ teaspoon salt
2 teaspoons vanilla extract	¾ cup milk

Cream butter or margarine until light and fluffy. Slowly beat in sugar and cream well. Add beaten egg yolks and vanilla. Add sifted dry ingredients alternately with milk. Fold in beaten egg whites. Pour into two greased 8-inch cake pans. Bake at 375° for 25 minutes.

❦ Imperial Cake

(BUNDT OR TUBE PAN)

1 pound butter (no substitute)	2 cups finely chopped
2 cups sugar	blanched almonds
9 eggs	¼ cup finely chopped citron
4 cups all-purpose flour	1 lemon, grated rind and juice

Cream butter and sugar (twice as long as you think necessary). Add whole eggs, one at a time, beating after each addition. (If by hand, beat 20 minutes; if by electric mixer at low speed, a shorter beating time may be used.) Sift flour and add to butter-egg mixture a little at a time. Mix chopped almonds and citron, lemon rind, and juice; fold into batter with spoon. Pour batter into greased round tube pan and bake at 300° for about 1½ hours. Keep cake a week before using.

❦ Honey Cake

(TWO 9-INCH LAYER PANS)

1 cup butter or margarine	½ teaspoon salt
2 cups honey	1 teaspoon ground ginger
2 eggs, beaten	1 teaspoon ground cinnamon
4 cups all-purpose flour	1 cup sour milk
2 teaspoons soda	

Cream butter thoroughly; gradually add honey, and beat into creamed butter until fluffy. Add beaten eggs and blend well. Combine dry ingredients. Add to creamed mixture alternately with sour milk. Put batter in two greased 9-inch layer pans. Bake at 275° for 35 to 40 minutes, or until cake tests done. (Watch carefully, as honey mixtures burn easily.) Frost as desired.

❦ Graham Cracker Cake

(THREE 9-INCH LAYER PANS)

1 pound box graham crackers	2 cups sugar
2 teaspoons baking powder	5 eggs
½ teaspoon salt	2 teaspoons vanilla extract
2 sticks butter or margarine	1 cup milk

Roll graham crackers to fine crumbs, combine with baking powder and salt and set aside. Cream butter or margarine, add sugar and beat until smooth. Add eggs, one at a time, beating well after each addition. Add vanilla. Add graham cracker mixture to creamed mixture alternately with milk. Put batter in three 9-inch layer cake pans lined with waxed paper which has been greased. Bake at 350° for 35 minutes, or until cake tests done. Cool, and frost with Pineapple Frosting.

❧ Lady Cake

(THREE 9-INCH LAYER PANS)

4 egg whites	½ cup butter
2 cups all-purpose flour	1½ cups sugar
½ teaspoon soda	Nearly 1 cup milk
1 teaspoon cream of tartar	Peach or almond flavoring

Let the egg whites warm to room temperature before using. Sift flour, measure, add soda and cream of tartar, and sift together three times. Cream butter, add sugar, and cream until well blended. Add flour alternately with the milk. Add flavoring and fold in stiffly beaten egg whites. Pour into three greased 9-inch layer cake pans. Bake at 325° for 15 minutes, then increase heat to 350° and bake 10 or 15 minutes longer.

❧ Crunchy-Top Cake

(10-INCH TUBE PAN)

1½ cups vegetable shortening	Juice of 1 lemon
3 cups sugar	1 teaspoon vanilla extract
9 egg yolks	9 egg whites, beaten
3 cups sifted cake flour	

Cream shortening and sugar until light and fluffy. Add egg yolks and flour alternately to creamed mixture. Add lemon juice and vanilla. Fold in beaten egg whites. Bake in a greased 10-inch tube pan at 325° for 1 hour and 10 minutes.

❦ Italian Cream Cake

(THREE 8-INCH LAYER PANS)

1 stick margarine	1 cup buttermilk
½ cup vegetable shortening	1 teaspoon vanilla extract
2 cups sugar	1 small can angel flake
5 egg yolks	coconut
2 cups all-purpose flour	1 cup chopped nuts
1 teaspoon soda	5 egg whites, stiffly beaten

Cream margarine and shortening; add sugar and beat until mixture is smooth. Add egg yolks and beat well. Combine flour and soda and add to creamed mixture alternately with buttermilk. Stir in vanilla. Add coconut and chopped nuts. Fold in stiffly beaten egg whites. Pour batter into three greased and floured 8-inch cake pans. Bake at 350° for 25 minutes or until cake tests done; cool. Frost with Cream Cheese Frosting.

❦ Lazy-Dazy Cake

(8- OR 9-INCH LAYER PAN)

2 eggs	1 teaspoon baking powder
1 cup sugar	½ cup hot milk
1 teaspoon vanilla extract	1 tablespoon butter or
1 cup all-purpose flour	margarine
½ teaspoon salt	

Beat the eggs; add sugar gradually, and stir in vanilla. Sift flour, salt, and baking powder and add them next, still beating. Scald milk and add the butter, allowing it to melt in the milk. Add this last and give a dozen more beats. Pour batter into greased 8- or 9-inch layer pan and bake at 350° for 30 to 35 minutes.

Broiled Topping

5 tablespoons butter, melted	½ cup coconut
9 tablespoons brown sugar	½ cup pecans
4 tablespoons cream	

Combine all ingredients. Pour over cake after it is baked and put under the broiler. Allow to broil until it bubbles and is slightly brown. Cut in squares and serve either hot or cold with ice cream on top.

ະ Cherry-Nut Cake

(TWO 9-INCH LAYER PANS)

1 (8-ounce) bottle maraschino
   cherries, drained and
   chopped
3 cups all-purpose flour
4 teaspoons baking powder
1 teaspoon salt
1½ teaspoons vanilla extract
   Water

¾ cups butter or margarine
1½ cups sugar
¼ teaspoon almond extract
¾ cup chopped nuts (walnuts
   or pecans)
4 egg whites, beaten

Drain cherries, reserving liquid. Add water to cherry juice to make 1 cup liquid. Chop cherries. Cream butter and sugar. Add 3 tablespoons cherry liquid and continue creaming until light and fluffy. Combine dry ingredients. Add to creamed mixture alternately with liquid, mixing thoroughly after each addition. Add vanilla and almond extract, nuts, and cherries. Fold stiffly beaten egg whites into batter. Pour batter into two 9-inch layer cake pans, lined with waxed paper. Bake at 350° for 25 minutes. Cool and frost with Never Fail Frosting.

ະ Peach Tart Viennese

(12-INCH PIZZA PAN)

¼ cup butter or margarine
¼ cup powdered sugar
1 cup sifted all-purpose flour
1 tablespoon cornstarch
2 tablespoons sugar

¼ teaspoon ground mace
½ cup orange juice
½ cup currant jelly, melted
8 large fresh peaches
   Whipped cream

Cream butter and powdered sugar (adding sugar gradually and creaming constantly); then add flour, mixing to form soft dough. Pat on bottom and sides of a 12-inch pizza pan. Bake in 350° oven for 20 minutes.

Combine cornstarch, sugar, mace, and orange juice in a saucepan. Cook over very low heat until thick and clear, stirring constantly. Stir in melted currant jelly. Allow to cool slightly. While glaze is cooling, peel, slice, and arrange peaches in a single layer in the baked pie shell. Spoon the glaze evenly over the peaches. Chill in refrigerator. Garnish with whipped cream before serving. Yield: 6 to 8 servings.

❦ Lord Baltimore Cake

(THREE 9-INCH LAYER PANS)

¾ cup butter	½ teaspoon salt
1¼ cups sugar	3 teaspoons baking powder
8 egg yolks, beaten	¾ cup milk
2½ cups cake flour	½ teaspoon lemon extract

Cream butter thoroughly, gradually add sugar, and cream together until fluffy. Beat egg yolks until very thick and light colored. Add to creamed mixture and beat for 5 to 10 minutes. Sift dry ingredients together and add to creamed mixture alternately with milk in small amounts at a time, beating well after each addition. Add lemon extract and beat vigorously. Put batter in three greased 9-inch layer cake pans and bake at 375° about 20 minutes. Cool. Spread Lord Baltimore Filling between layers and cover top and sides with Divinity Frosting.

❦ Charleston Lord Baltimore Cake

(THREE 9-INCH LAYER PANS)

2¾ cups all-purpose flour	1¼ cups sugar
2¼ teaspoons baking powder	8 egg yolks
½ teaspoon salt	¼ cup milk
¼ cup butter	½ teaspoon lemon extract

Sift flour once, measure, add baking powder and salt, and sift together three times. Cream butter thoroughly, add sugar gradually, and cream together until light and fluffy. Beat egg yolks very thoroughly until light colored and thick enough to fall from beater in heavy continuous stream. Add to creamed mixture and beat until very smooth, almost waxy in appearance. Add flour, alternately with milk, a small amount at a time, beating very thoroughly after each addition. When all flour is added, beat thoroughly again. Add lemon extract. Bake in three greased 9-inch layer pans at 375° about 25 minutes or until done. Spread Lord Baltimore Frosting between layers and on top of cake.

❦ Lady Baltimore Cake

(THREE 9-INCH LAYER PANS)

3 cups sifted cake flour	½ cup milk
3 teaspoons baking powder	½ cup water
½ teaspoon salt	1 teaspoon vanilla extract
¾ cup shortening	6 egg whites, beaten
2 cups sugar	

Sift flour, baking powder, and salt. Cream shortening with sugar until fluffy. Combine milk, water, and vanilla. Add sifted dry ingredients to creamed mixture alternately with liquids. Beat egg whites until stiff, but not dry. Fold whites into batter. Pour batter into three greased 9-inch layer cake pans, and bake at 350° for 25 minutes. Cool. Spread Lady Baltimore Filling between layers and cover top and sides with Seven-Minute Frosting.

❦ Charleston Lady Baltimore Cake

(TWO 9-INCH LAYER PANS)

½ cup butter or margarine	2 teaspoons baking powder
1 cup sugar	½ cup milk
1¾ cups all-purpose flour	1 teaspoon vanilla extract
⅛ teaspoon salt	3 egg whites

Cream butter or margarine. Add sugar and cream again thoroughly. Sift dry ingredients and add alternately with milk. Add vanilla and fold in stiffly beaten egg whites. Bake in two layers at 350° for 25 minutes. Put layers together with Lady Baltimore Filling. There are many variations. Some recipes call for covering cake with a thick syrup made of 1 cup sugar, 1½ cups water. This is put on as soon as cakes are removed from pan. A white frosting is then put on top of syrup mixture.

❧ Kiss Cakes

(COOKIE SHEET)

4 egg whites	1 teaspoon vanilla extract
2 cups fine, granulated sugar	3 drops almond extract
1 tablespoon cornstarch	1 cup broken pecans
Dash of salt	

Beat the egg whites very stiff; add sugar a little at a time, stirring in with a fork. It is very important to add only a little bit of sugar at a time, beginning as the eggs pile up and taking plenty of time and thought as you go. Sprinkle in the cornstarch and the salt. Add the flavorings. Next add the pecans, sprinkling in a few at a time. Drop mixture by the tablespoonfuls on brown paper; place on a cookie sheet and bake at 350° for 45 minutes. They are done when you can lift them from the paper. This is a famous party cookie, served often with fruit punch at large gatherings. Yield: 2½ dozen cookies.

❧ Oatmeal Cake

(13- x 9- x 2-INCH PAN)

1¼ cups boiling water	2 eggs
1 cup oats (quick-cooking or regular)	1⅓ cups all-purpose flour
1 stick butter or margarine	1 teaspoon ground cinnamon
1 cup brown sugar	1 teaspoon soda
1 cup white sugar	1 teaspoon salt

Mix boiling water and oats and let stand 20 minutes. Cream together shortening and sugar. Add eggs and beat well. Add oats mixture. Add dry ingredients and mix well. Bake in a greased 13- x 9- x 2-inch pan at 275° for 35 to 45 minutes. While still warm, put Topping on cake and return to oven to broil for about 5 minutes.

Topping for Oatmeal Cake

1 cup light brown sugar
1 stick butter or margarine
¼ cup cream
1 cup coconut

Mix all ingredients and spread on cake. Place under broiler for 5 minutes.

❧ Praline Cake

(TWO 8-INCH LAYER PANS)

½ cup shortening	2 cups all-purpose flour
1½ cups sugar	2½ teaspoons baking powder
1 teaspoon vanilla extract	1 teaspoon salt
2 eggs	1 cup plus 2 tablespoons milk

Cream shortening until soft. Gradually add sugar and cream thoroughly (15 to 18 minutes in mixer). Add vanilla. Add eggs, one at a time, and beat well after each. Combine flour, baking powder, and salt; add to creamed mixture alternately with milk, beating constantly. Bake in two greased 8-inch layer cake pans at 375° for 25 minutes. Prepare Topping while cake is baking.

Topping

½ cup butter	2 eggs, beaten
1 (1-pound) package light brown sugar	1 teaspoon vanilla extract
2 tablespoons all-purpose flour	1½ cups pecans, broken

Melt butter in a skillet. Mix brown sugar, flour, and eggs. Add to the melted butter in skillet and cook for 3 minutes over low heat. Remove from heat, stir in vanilla and pecans. Spread evenly over the surface of the cakes. Return cakes to oven and bake at 400° for 8 minutes to "set" the frosting. Cool.

❧ Grape Cake

(TWO 9-INCH LAYER PANS)

½ cup vegetable shortening	3 teaspoons baking powder
¾ teaspoon salt	½ cup milk
1½ teaspoons vanilla extract	½ cup water
1½ cups sugar	4 egg whites, stiffly beaten
2¾ cups all-purpose flour	

Blend shortening, salt, and vanilla. Add sugar and cream well. Sift dry ingredients and add to creamed mixture alternately with milk and water. Mix after each addition until smooth. Fold in beaten egg whites. Bake in two 9-inch greased and floured layer cake pans at 350° for 25 minutes.

❦ Chess Cake

(13- x 9- x 2-INCH PAN)

2 sticks margarine
1 box brown sugar
1 cup granulated sugar
4 egg yolks
2 cups all-purpose flour
2 teaspoons baking powder
¼ teaspoon salt
1 cup broken nuts (optional)
1½ teaspoons vanilla extract
4 egg whites
Powdered sugar

Melt margarine, add both sugars, and blend well. Add egg yolks and beat well. Sift flour, baking powder, and salt; add to creamed mixture. Fold in nuts and vanilla. Beat egg whites until stiff; fold into creamed mixture. Spread batter in greased and floured 13- x 9- x 2-inch pan and bake at 350° for 30 to 45 minutes. When done, sprinkle with powdered sugar.

❦ Moravian Sugar Cake

(13- x 9- x 2-INCH PAN)

1 package dry yeast
½ cup very warm water
1 cup unseasoned mashed
  potatoes
1 cup sugar
4 tablespoons soft butter
½ cup shortening
1 teaspoon salt
1 cup potato water
1 cup all-purpose flour
2 eggs, beaten
  About 3½ cups all-purpose
  flour
Brown sugar
Cinnamon

Allow yeast to soften in water. To the hot, unseasoned mashed potatoes add sugar, butter, shortening, and salt. When lukewarm, add yeast mixture and potato water. Add 1 cup flour. Allow to rise until spongy. Add two beaten eggs and enough flour to make a soft dough (about 3½ cups). Allow to rise until doubled in bulk. Punch down on lightly floured board.

Spread out evenly in greased 13- x 9- x 2-inch baking pan. Cover and let rise. When "light," make holes in dough with your fingers and fill holes with pieces of butter and brown sugar. Dust with cinnamon. Bake at 375° for 20 minutes. Cut into squares and serve hot or cold.

❦ Petits Fours

(15½- x 10½- x 1-INCH JELLYROLL PAN)

2¼ cups cake flour
1½ cups sugar
3½ teaspoons baking powder
1 teaspoon salt
½ cup soft shortening

1 cup milk
1 teaspoon vanilla extract
4 egg whites (½ to ⅔ cup), unbeaten

Blend flour, sugar, baking powder, and salt. Add shortening, ⅔ cup milk, and vanilla. Beat 2 minutes at medium speed on mixer or 300 vigorous strokes by hand. Scrape sides and bottom of bowl constantly. Add rest of milk and egg whites. Beat 2 minutes more, scraping bowl frequently. Pour into greased and floured 15½- x 10½- x 1-inch jellyroll pan. Bake at 350° about 25 minutes. Cool in pan. Cut into fancy shapes or 1½-inch squares. Frost upside down so crust is on bottom. Stick fork into bottom of petits fours and hold over pan while spooning frosting over sides of cake. To frost tops, set cake on cooling rack over large bowl. Pour Petits Fours Frosting over tops so entire cake is covered at one time (pour from small cup). Decorate as desired.

❦ Rum Cake

(TWO 8- x 8- x 2-INCH PANS)

1 cup butter
2 cups sugar
3½ cups sifted cake flour
8 egg whites, stiffly beaten

1 cup milk
3½ teaspoons baking powder
1 teaspoon vanilla extract
Pinch salt

Cream butter; gradually add sugar and continue creaming until smooth. Sift flour; measure and keep out 2 tablespoons. To the creamed mixture, add rest of flour, egg whites, and milk alternately in thirds. Beat well after each addition.

Next mix the baking powder with the 2 tablespoons flour and add after the cake is thoroughly mixed. Beat vigorously. Add vanilla and salt last. Bake in two greased 8- x 8- x 2-inch layer cake pans at 350° about 20 to 30 minutes. Put layers together with Rum Filling and frost with your favorite frosting, using rum for flavoring.

❧ Maclamation Cake

(TWO 8- OR 9-INCH LAYER PANS)

2¼ cups sifted cake flour
1½ cups sugar
3½ teaspoons baking powder
1 teaspoon salt
½ cup soft shortening

1 cup milk, divided
1 teaspoon flavoring
4 egg whites (½ to ⅔ cup),
    beaten

Combine flour, sugar, baking powder, and salt in bowl. Add shortening, ⅔ cup milk, and flavoring. Add remaining ⅓ cup milk and stiffly beaten egg whites. Beat 2 minutes longer. Pour into two 8- or 9-inch greased layer cake pans. Bake at 350° 30 to 35 minutes. Put layers together with Maclamation Filling and frost with a white frosting.

❧ Special Cake

(13- x 9- x 2-INCH PAN)

2 cups crushed pineapple and
    juice
1½ cups grated coconut
1 cup pecans, if desired

1 box yellow cake mix
2 sticks margarine, sliced in
    ¼-inch squares

Pour crushed pineapple and juice into a greased 13- x 9- x 2-inch pan or two 8-inch pans. Cover with coconut and pecans (if desired). Spread dry cake mix over mixture. Place squares of margarine over entire top of cake. Bake at 350° for about 25 minutes or until brown. Serve with ice cream or whipped cream.

❧ Queen Elizabeth Cake

(13- x 9- x 2-INCH PAN)

1 cup boiling water
1 cup chopped pitted dates
1 teaspoon soda
¼ cup butter or margarine
1 cup sugar
1 egg, beaten

1 tablespoon vanilla extract
3 cups all-purpose flour
1 teaspoon baking powder
⅓ teaspoon salt
⅓ cup chopped nuts

Pour boiling water over dates, add soda, and let stand until cool. Cream butter or margarine, add sugar, and stir until well mixed. Add beaten egg and vanilla. Add sifted dry ingredients, and nuts; and mix well. Add the cooled dates and water. Bake in a greased 13- x 9- x 2-inch pan at 325° for 35 to 45 minutes.

❧ Sunshine Cake

(10-INCH TUBE PAN)

12 egg yolks	¼ teaspoon salt
2 cups sugar	1 teaspoon vanilla extract
2 cups all-purpose flour	1 cup hot water
2 teaspoons baking powder	

Beat egg yolks; add sugar, and beat until thoroughly mixed. Sift together flour, baking powder, and salt and beat slowly into egg and sugar mixture. Add vanilla. Add hot water slowly with mixer set on slow speed. This makes a thin batter; but do not worry, for the egg yolks thicken it as it bakes. Bake in a greased and floured tube pan at 325° about 1 hour.

❧ One-Two-Three-Four Cake

(THREE 9-INCH LAYER PANS)

1 cup butter	3 teaspoons baking powder
2 cups sugar	1 cup milk
4 egg yolks, beaten	1 teaspoon vanilla extract
3 cups all-purpose flour	4 egg whites, beaten
1 teaspoon salt	

Beat the butter and sugar till very light and creamy. Add the well-beaten egg yolks. Sift flour twice with salt and baking powder. Add to creamed mixture alternately with milk, a little at a time. Add vanilla. Fold in beaten egg whites. Put batter in three greased 9-inch layer cake pans. Bake at 350° for 30 minutes. Cover with favorite frosting.

Variation: One cup buttermilk and ½ teaspoon soda may be substituted for the sweet milk.

❧ Tutti-Frutti Loaf Cake

(LARGE LOAF PAN)

2¼ cups all-purpose flour
1¼ cups sugar
1½ teaspoons baking powder
1 teaspoon salt
½ cup soft shortening
½ cup milk
1 teaspoon vanilla extract

4 egg whites (½ cup), beaten
¼ cup chopped nuts
1 cup chopped mixed candied
fruit
2 tablespoons all-purpose
flour

Combine first four dry ingredients in large bowl. Add shortening, milk, and vanilla; beat well. Add egg whites and beat an additional 2 minutes. Fold in nuts and fruits which have been coated with 2 tablespoons flour. Bake in a large greased loaf pan at 350° for 60 to 65 minutes or until cake tests done.

❧ Whisper Cake

(13- x 9- x 2-INCH PAN)

1 package fruit-flavored gelatin
⅔ cup hot water
4 eggs
⅔ cup salad oil

1 package white or yellow
cake mix
1 can flaked coconut
1 cup chopped pecans

Dissolve gelatin in hot water. Beat eggs and oil together in large bowl. Add cake mix and mix well. Add dissolved gelatin. Mix. Put batter into greased 13- x 9- x 2-inch pan and bake at 350° until cake is nearly done (about 30 to 35 minutes). Remove from oven and sprinkle coconut and pecans over cake.

Frosting

1½ cups sugar
1 cup buttermilk
1 teaspoon soda

2 tablespoons melted butter or
margarine

For frosting, mix together sugar, buttermilk, soda, and butter. Pour over hot cake and bake until coconut browns. (When putting frosting on cake, allow some of it to run down sides of the pan.)

❦ Spice Cake With Meringue

(13- x 9- x 2-INCH PAN)

¾ cup shortening
2 cups brown sugar
2 beaten egg yolks
2⅓ cups all-purpose flour
¾ teaspoon salt

1 teaspoon baking powder
1 teaspoon ground cloves
1 teaspoon ground cinnamon
1 teaspoon soda in 1¼ cups
    buttermilk
1 teaspoon vanilla extract

Cream shortening and sugar. Add egg yolks and beat until fluffy. Sift dry ingredients together; add to creamed mixture alternately with milk, beating after each addition. Add vanilla. Pour into greased and floured 13- x 9- x 2-inch pan.

Meringue

2 egg whites
1 cup brown sugar
½ cup chopped nuts

Beat egg whites; add sugar gradually as in other meringues. Spread over batter. Sprinkle with nuts. Bake at 325° about 50 minutes. Cut in squares to serve.

❦ Sweet Potato Surprise Cake

(THREE 8-INCH LAYER PANS)

1½ cups cooking oil
2 cups sugar
4 eggs, separated
4 tablespoons hot water
2½ cups sifted cake flour
3 teaspoons baking powder

1 teaspoon ground cinnamon
1 teaspoon ground nutmeg
1½ cups grated raw sweet
    potatoes
1 cup chopped nuts
1 teaspoon vanilla extract

Combine cooking oil and sugar and beat until smooth. Add egg yolks and beat well. Add hot water, then dry ingredients which have been sifted together. Stir in potatoes, nuts, and vanilla and beat well. Beat egg whites until stiff and fold into mixture. Bake in three greased 8-inch layer cake pans at 350° for 25 to 30 minutes. Cool and frost with Sweet Chocolate Filling

Note: To freeze, wrap before frosting in moisture-vaporproof material.

❦ Tomato Soup Cake

(10-INCH TUBE PAN)

¾ cups butter or margarine	1½ teaspoons ground cinnamon
1½ cups sugar	1½ teaspoons ground nutmeg
3 cups all-purpose flour	1 cup condensed tomato soup
¾ teaspoon salt	¾ cup water
3 teaspoons baking powder	1½ cups raisins
1 teaspoon ground cloves	1½ cups chopped nuts

Cream the butter and slowly add the sugar. Sift together the dry ingredients and add alternately to the creamed mixture with the tomato soup which has been combined with the water. Mix thoroughly. Add the raisins and nuts and pour into a well-greased tube pan. Bake at 350° for 1 hour. Cool and frost with Cream Cheese Frosting.

❦ Sour Cream Loaf Cake

(LOAF PAN)

2 eggs	½ teaspoon vanilla extract
1 cup sugar	2 cups all-purpose flour
½ teaspoon soda	2 teaspoons baking powder
1 cup commercial sour cream	½ teaspoon salt

Beat the eggs until light. Add the sugar and beat again. Dissolve the soda in the sour cream, stirring thoroughly, then add to the egg mixture with the vanilla. Combine flour, baking powder, and salt. Add to creamed mixture and stir until blended. Pour into a greased loaf pan and bake at 350° for 50 minutes.

❦ Vanilla French Cream Cake

(9-INCH SPRINGFORM PAN)

3 eggs	1 cup sifted cake flour
1 cup sugar	1 teaspoon baking powder
3 tablespoons cold water	⅛ teaspoon salt
1½ teaspoons vanilla extract	

Beat eggs until light and lemon colored (about 5 minutes with electric beater). Gradually beat in sugar and beat until the mixture is thick and pale. Blend in water and vanilla. Sift flour with baking powder and salt three times. Stir into the mixture. Pour batter into an ungreased 9-inch springform pan. Bake at 350° for 40 minutes, or until cake tester inserted in center comes out clean. Cool cake in pan. Top with Vanilla Cream Frosting.

☙ Ten-Dollar Cake

(THREE 9-INCH LAYER PANS)

1 cup butter	¼ teaspoon salt
2½ cups sugar	1 cup buttermilk
4 egg yolks	5 teaspoons strong coffee
3 cups all-purpose flour	1 teaspoon vanilla extract
1 teaspoon soda	1 teaspoon lemon extract
3 teaspoons cocoa	5 egg whites, beaten

Cream butter and sugar together until fluffy; add egg yolks, one at a time, and beat well. Sift together flour, soda, cocoa, and salt; add buttermilk and flour alternately to creamed mixture. Add coffee and extracts and mix well. Fold in egg whites. Bake in three greased 9-inch pans at 350° for 30 to 35 minutes. Frost as desired.

☙ Velvet Cake

(LOAF PAN)

1 cup butter	2 cups all-purpose flour
1½ cups sugar	1 teaspoon vanilla extract
5 eggs	

Cream butter and sugar until light and fluffy. Add eggs, one at a time, beating well after each addition. Add small amount of flour between each egg. Add vanilla. Bake in greased loaf pan at 350° for 45 to 50 minutes. May be covered with powdered sugar frosting, if desired.

❦ Silver Cake

(TWO 8-INCH LAYER PANS)

2¼ cups sifted cake flour	¾ cup milk
1⅓ cups sugar	4 egg whites
1 teaspoon salt	⅓ cup milk
3½ teaspoons baking powder	1 teaspoon vanilla extract
½ cup vegetable shortening	

Combine flour, sugar, salt, and baking powder in mixing bowl. Add shortening and the first milk called for in recipe. Beat vigorously by hand or electric mixer, at medium speed for 2 minutes. Add egg whites, additional milk, and vanilla.

Beat for 2 minutes. Pour into two 8-inch layer pans which have been lined with plain paper, or rubbed with vegetable shortening and floured. Bake at 350° for 30 minutes. Frost.

❦ "Rush Up" Cake

(13- x 9- x 2-INCH PAN)

¾ cup shortening	2⅓ cups all-purpose flour
2 cups brown sugar	1 teaspoon baking powder
2 eggs, separated	1 teaspoon ground cloves
1 teaspoon soda	1 teaspoon ground cinnamon
1¼ cups sour milk	1 teaspoon vanilla extract

Cream together shortening, sugar, and egg yolks. Dissolve soda in sour milk and add alternately with all dry ingredients. Add vanilla. Mix until smooth, and pour into greased 13- x 9- x 2-inch pan. Cover with Brown Sugar Meringue. Bake at 350° for 40 minutes.

Brown Sugar Meringue

2 egg whites (left over from cake)	½ cup nuts
1 cup brown sugar	

Beat egg whites until stiff. Slowly add brown sugar and beat until smooth. Add nuts. Spread on cake batter and bake.

❧ Dutch Funny Cake

(9-INCH PIE PLATE)

Pastry for 9- or 10-inch pie plate
1¼ cups cake flour
1 teaspoon baking powder
½ teaspoon salt
¾ cup sugar
¼ cup shortening
½ cup milk
1 teaspoon vanilla extract
1 egg, unbeaten

Line pie plate with pastry, making a high fluted rim. Make a Sauce (recipes below); let cool while mixing cake.

Have all ingredients for cake at room temperature. Sift flour; combine flour, baking powder, salt, and sugar. Place shortening in large bowl. Sift in dry ingredients. Add milk and vanilla; mix until flour is dampened. Beat 2 minutes with mixer or 300 strokes by hand. Add egg and beat 1 minute longer. Pour batter into pastry-lined pie plate. Pour lukewarm sauce gently over the batter. Sprinkle with nuts or coconut. Bake at 350° for 50 to 55 minutes.

Chocolate Sauce

Place 1 square unsweetened chocolate and ½ cup water in pan over low heat. Cook and stir until chocolate is melted. Add ⅔ cup sugar, stirring constantly, and then bring to a boil. Remove from heat at once; add ¼ cup butter or margarine and 1 teaspoon vanilla extract and blend.

Butterscotch Sauce

In a pan, combine ¼ cup butter or margarine with ½ cup firmly packed brown sugar and 2 tablespoons light corn syrup. Cook and stir over low heat until mixture comes to a boil. Add 3 tablespoons water and bring to a boil again. Boil 1 to 2 minutes. Remove from heat and stir in ½ teaspoon vanilla extract.

Orange Sauce

Combine ¼ cup orange juice and ¾ cup sugar in pan. Place over low heat; cook and stir until mixture comes to a boil. Boil 1 minute, stirring constantly. Then add ¼ cup orange juice, 2 tablespoons butter or margarine, and 1 teaspoon grated orange rind. Mix well.

❦ Vanilla Wafer Cake

(TUBE PAN)

1 cup margarine or butter	½ cup milk
2 cups sugar	1 (7-ounce) package flaked
6 whole eggs	coconut
1 (12-ounce) box vanilla	1 cup chopped pecans
wafers	

Cream margarine or butter, add sugar, and beat until smooth. Add eggs, one at a time, beating well after each addition. Add vanilla wafers, which have been crushed, alternately with milk. Add coconut and pecans. Pour batter into a greased and floured tube pan. Bake at 275° for 1½ hours.

❦ Yum-Yum Cake

(13- x 9- x 2-INCH PAN)

2 eggs	2 cups all-purpose flour
2 cups sugar	2½ teaspoons baking powder
2 cups crushed pineapple (do	Topping
not drain)	

Beat eggs and sugar together until light and fluffy. Stir in pineapple. Add flour which has been sifted with baking powder. Mix well and spread batter into a greased and floured 13- x 9- x 2-inch pan; bake at 350° for 25 to 30 minutes or until cake tests done. Add Topping.

Topping

1 cup sugar	1 cup flaked coconut
1 stick margarine	1 cup chopped pecans
1 (5⅓-ounce) can evaporated	½ teaspoon vanilla extract
milk	½ teaspoon lemon extract

Put sugar, margarine, and milk in saucepan; boil for 2 minutes. Remove from heat and add coconut, pecans, and vanilla and lemon extracts. Spread over hot cake.

Section Three

Frosting and Filling Recipes

❧ Speedy Banana Frosting

¼ cup butter or margarine   ½ cup mashed ripe bananas
1 pound powdered sugar   1 teaspoon lemon juice

Cream butter until soft and fluffy. Add half the sugar and beat until blended. Add mashed bananas and lemon juice. Add remaining sugar and beat until frosting is of spreading consistency.

❧ Black Walnut Frosting

2 cups light brown sugar   2 egg whites, stiffly beaten
½ cup water   Finely ground black walnuts
½ cup light corn syrup

Cook sugar, water, and corn syrup over medium heat until it spins a thread. Pour syrup over beaten egg whites and continue beating until of consistency to spread. Spread between layers and on top and sides of cake. Sprinkle finely ground walnuts over cake.

❧ Butter Frosting

2 cups sugar   ¼ teaspoon salt
1 cup butter or margarine   1 teaspoon vanilla extract
1 cup milk

Put all ingredients except vanilla in heavy saucepan and boil until it will form a soft ball when a small amount is dropped from spoon into cold water. Remove from heat and add vanilla. Beat until thick and creamy.

Brown Sugar Frosting

1 stick margarine
1 cup brown sugar
¼ cup milk

3 cups powdered sugar
1 teaspoon vanilla extract

Melt margarine on medium heat. Add brown sugar and stir 1 minute. Add milk, powdered sugar, and vanilla and blend until creamy.

Brownstone Front Cake Frosting

2 cups sugar
2 sticks margarine

1 (5⅓-ounce) can evaporated milk
1 teaspoon vanilla extract

Combine sugar, margarine, and evaporated milk. Cook about 20 minutes, or until it forms a soft ball in cold water. Add vanilla. Beat until right consistency to spread.

Browned Butter Frosting

⅓ cup soft butter
3 cups sifted powdered sugar

3 tablespoons cream
1½ teaspoons vanilla extract

Heat butter in saucepan over medium heat until delicate brown. Blend butter and sugar together. Stir in cream and vanilla and mix until smooth. Frosting can be garnished with walnuts, if desired.

Uncooked Butter Icing

1 tablespoon butter or margarine
2 cups sifted powdered sugar

Grated rind of 1 lemon
Juice of 1 lemon

Melt butter or margarine and add sugar, grated rind, and lemon juice. Beat well. Add milk, if needed, to make frosting of spreading consistency. Yield: enough for one 8- or 9-inch layer.

❦ Mardi Gras Filling

½ cup sugar
1 tablespoon cornstarch
½ cup evaporated milk
⅓ cup butterscotch pieces
1 egg yolk, beaten

2 tablespoons butter
1 cup flaked coconut
1 cup chopped pecans or
  walnuts

Combine sugar and cornstarch in 2-quart saucepan. Stir in milk, butterscotch pieces, and egg yolk. Cook over medium heat, stirring constantly, until thick. Remove from heat, add butter, coconut, and nuts. Cool.

❦ Butterscotch Delight Frosting

1 (6-ounce) package
  butterscotch pieces
2 tablespoons water
1 (8-ounce) package cream
  cheese

1 tablespoon light cream
¼ teaspoon salt
1 teaspoon vanilla extract
1 cup heavy cream, whipped

Melt butterscotch pieces over hot (not boiling) water. Add water, and stir until blended. Remove from heat and cool to lukewarm. Combine cream cheese, light cream, and salt and beat until light. Blend in melted butterscotch and vanilla. Fold in whipped cream and spread on cake.

❦ Old-Fashioned Caramel Frosting

4 cups white sugar
1 cup milk

1 tablespoon butter or
  margarine

Put 3 cups of the sugar and the milk in a saucepan and bring to a boil. In a large, heavy skillet place the other cup of sugar and cook until sugar is caramelized, stirring constantly. Add the hot syrup mixture to the caramelized sugar, stirring constantly. Add the butter or margarine, and cook until it reaches the soft ball stage (238° to 240°). Remove from heat and beat until creamy. Yield: enough for two 9-inch layers.

❧ Caramel Frosting

¾ cup sugar   1 stick butter or margarine
¾ cup milk   1 teaspoon vanilla extract
2 cups sugar

Caramelize the ¾ cup sugar in heavy skillet. Do not stir. Combine milk and 2 cups sugar in another large skillet or heavy saucepan. Bring to a rolling boil. Gradually add caramelized sugar and cook to the soft ball stage. Add butter and vanilla. Cool slightly and beat to spreading consistency.

❧ Brown Sugar Caramel Frosting

3 cups brown sugar   1 teaspoon vanilla extract
1 cup water   Cream or rich milk, to soften
1 tablespoon butter or
    margarine

Boil the sugar and water until the syrup reaches the soft ball stage (238° to 240°). Add the butter or margarine and vanilla and remove from heat. Let cool, then beat until thick and creamy. Add cream until of consistency to spread. Yield: enough for two 9-inch layers.

❧ White Caramel Frosting

2½ cups sugar   1 cup raisins, if desired
¾ cup butter or margarine   1 cup chopped pecans
1 cup milk

Mix sugar, butter, and milk in saucepan. Stir constantly over low heat until sugar is dissolved and butter melted. Continue to boil until small amount forms a soft ball when dropped in cold water. Remove from heat. Add raisins and pecans, if desired. Beat until creamy. Yield: enough to fill and frost two 8- or 9-inch layers.

❦ Frosting for Carrot Cake

1 box powdered sugar	½ stick margarine
1 (8-ounce) package cream cheese	1 teaspoon lemon extract

Mix all ingredients together until smooth and spread on cake. Yield: enough for three 9-inch layers.

❦ Chocolate Frosting

¼ cup butter or margarine	1 square unsweetened
3½ cups sifted powdered sugar	chocolate, melted
3 tablespoons milk	

Cream butter or margarine and sugar. Add milk and melted chocolate and beat until blended. Yield: enough for three 8-inch layers.

❦ Quick Chocolate Frosting

2 squares unsweetened chocolate	1 tablespoon water
1 (15-ounce) can sweetened condensed milk	Dash of salt
	½ teaspoon vanilla extract

Melt the chocolate in the top of a double boiler. Add the condensed milk gradually, mixing well. Then add the water and salt and blend. Cook for 5 minutes over rapidly boiling water, stirring constantly. Remove from heat and add vanilla. Cool. Yield: enough for tops of two 9-inch layers.

❦ Easy Chocolate Frosting

1 stick butter or margarine	⅔ cup evaporated milk
⅓ cup cocoa	1 teaspoon vanilla extract
¼ teaspoon salt	2 cups sugar

Melt butter slowly in heavy saucepan. Add other ingredients except vanilla and boil 3 minutes. Add vanilla and cool. Beat to spreading consistency.

❦ Chocolate Fudge Frosting

¼ pound butter or margarine	½ cup milk
1½ squares unsweetened chocolate	2 cups sugar
	1 teaspoon vanilla extract

Put all ingredients except vanilla into saucepan. Stir over medium heat until sugar is dissolved. Boil 2½ minutes. Remove from heat, add vanilla, cool, and beat.

❦ Hungarian Chocolate Frosting

3 squares unsweetened chocolate	3 egg yolks
1½ cups sifted powdered sugar	4 tablespoons butter
2¼ tablespoons hot water	

Melt chocolate in double boiler. Remove from boiling water, add sugar and water, and blend. Add egg yolks, one at a time, beating well after each. Add butter, a tablespoon at a time, beating thoroughly after each addition. Yield: enough to cover top and sides of two 8- or 9-inch layers.

❦ Brown Beauty Frosting

1 (6-ounce) package semi-sweet chocolate pieces	½ cup strong coffee
1 (6-ounce) package butterscotch pieces	3 cups sifted powdered sugar

Melt chocolate and butterscotch pieces over hot water. Remove from heat and stir in coffee and sugar, beating until smooth. Yield: enough for three 9-inch layers.

❧ Honey-Chocolate Frosting

½ cup sugar
¼ cup butter or margarine
¼ cup light cream
¼ cup honey
¼ teaspoon salt

3 squares unsweetened
    chocolate, cut in small
    pieces
2 egg yolks, well beaten

Combine sugar, butter or margarine, cream, honey, salt, and chocolate in the top of a double boiler. Place over boiling water. When chocolate is melted, beat until well blended. Pour a small amount over the beaten egg yolks, stirring constantly. Return to double boiler and cook 2 minutes longer, or until the mixture thickens slightly, stirring constantly. Remove from the hot water and set pan in ice water and beat until of right consistency to spread. Yield: enough for tops and sides of two 8-inch layers.

❧ White Chocolate Frosting

½ cup plus 2 tablespoons sugar
6 tablespoons evaporated milk
¼ cup butter or margarine
2 cups white chocolate, cut
    into small pieces

1½ teaspoons vanilla extract
Slivered toasted almonds or
    other nuts for garnish

Combine sugar, milk, and butter in a saucepan. Bring mixture to full rolling boil and boil 1 minute. Remove from heat and add white chocolate and vanilla. Stir until candy is melted; beat until smooth and of spreading consistency. Frost cake and garnish with nuts. Yield: enough for three 9-inch layers.

❧ Smooth Fudge Frosting

2 tablespoons shortening
2 tablespoons margarine
1 tablespoon corn syrup
2 squares unsweetened
    chocolate

7 tablespoons milk
1½ cups sugar
⅛ teaspoon salt
1 teaspoon vanilla extract

Combine all ingredients, except vanilla, in heavy saucepan. Bring to a rolling boil over low heat and boil 1 minute only. Cool. Add vanilla and beat until smooth. Yield: enough for two 8-inch layers.

Fudge Frosting

2 ounces unsweetened chocolate, finely cut
1½ cups sugar
7 tablespoons milk
2 tablespoons shortening

2 tablespoons butter or margarine
1 tablespoon corn syrup
¼ teaspoon salt
1 teaspoon vanilla extract

Place chocolate, sugar, milk, shortening, butter or margarine, corn syrup, and salt in a saucepan. Bring slowly to a full rolling boil, stirring constantly, and boil briskly for 1 minute (1½ minutes if the weather is damp). Remove from heat and cool to lukewarm. Add vanilla and beat until thick enough to spread. Yield: enough for tops of two 8-inch layers or top and sides of a 13- x 9- x 2-inch cake.

Chocolate Seven-Minute Frosting

2 egg whites, unbeaten
1½ cups sugar
1½ teaspoons light corn syrup
5 tablespoons cold water

1 teaspoon vanilla extract
3 squares unsweetened chocolate, melted

Put egg whites, sugar, corn syrup, and water in upper part of double boiler. Beat with rotary egg beater until thoroughly mixed. Place over rapidly boiling water, beat constantly, and cook for 7 minutes, or until frosting will stand in peaks. Remove from heat, add vanilla, and beat until thick enough to spread. Fold chocolate into frosting. (Do not beat mixture.) Cool and spread on cake. Yield: enough to cover two 9-inch layers.

❦ Mocha Frosting

½ square unsweetened chocolate,
    melted
2 tablespoons soft butter
2 cups powdered sugar

1 teaspoon vanilla extract
3 tablespoons strong hot
    coffee

Combine all ingredients; whip until light and fluffy. Add more coffee, if needed. Yield: enough for 13- x 9- x 2-inch sheet cake.

❦ Bittersweet Mocha Frosting

1 cup sugar
1 cup cocoa
¼ teaspoon salt

½ cup strong coffee
½ cup nuts, chopped
¼ teaspoon vanilla extract

Combine sugar, cocoa, and salt in a saucepan. Blend in the coffee. Cook over low heat until smooth and glossy, stirring often (takes about 15 minutes). Cool. Beat in nuts and vanilla. Chill until firm. Spread frosting with spatula dipped in hot water. Yield: enough for 24 tiny cup cakes or top and sides of one 9-inch layer.

❦ Cocoa-Mocha Frosting

6 tablespoons coffee
1 teaspoon vanilla extract
1 pound powdered sugar
1 cup sifted cocoa

½ teaspoon salt
6 tablespoons butter or
    margarine

Combine medium-strength, cold coffee and vanilla in mixing bowl. Sift sugar. Then sift all dry ingredients together. Add to liquids in three parts, beating until smooth after each addition. Gradually beat in soft butter or margarine, 1 tablespoonful at a time. Beat until smooth and creamy. Yield: enough for tops and sides of two 9-inch layers.

❧ Sweet Chocolate Filling

3 egg yolks
1 cup evaporated milk
1 cup sugar
1 tablespoon butter or
    margarine

1 cup flaked coconut
1 cup chopped nuts
1 teaspoon vanilla extract

Beat eggs and add milk, sugar, and butter or margarine. Cook over medium heat for 12 minutes, stirring constantly, until mixture thickens. Cool; add coconut, nuts, and vanilla, beating to spreading consistency. Spread between layers and on top of two-layer cake.

❧ Creamy Semi-Sweet Frosting

¼ cup butter or margarine
    Dash of salt
3 tablespoons milk
1 (6-ounce) package
    semi-sweet chocolate
    pieces

1 teaspoon vanilla extract
1 (7½-ounce) jar
    marshmallow cream

Combine the butter or margarine, salt, and milk in a saucepan and bring just to the boiling point. Remove from heat and add the chocolate pieces, stirring until smooth. Add vanilla. Let cool, then beat in the marshmallow cream until smooth. Yield: enough for two 8- or 9-inch layers.

❧ Semi-Sweet Quick Frosting

⅓ cup butter or margarine
⅔ cup evaporated milk
⅛ teaspoon salt
3 cups powdered sugar

1 (6-ounce) package
    semi-sweet chocolate
    pieces

Combine the butter or margarine, milk, and salt in a saucepan. Bring to the boiling point, stirring constantly. Remove from heat and add the chocolate pieces, stirring until smooth. Then gradually beat in the powdered sugar until thick enough to spread. Yield: enough for two 8-inch layers.

❦ Coconut Frosting

2 egg whites	½ teaspoon vanilla extract
1½ cups sugar	½ teaspoon coconut flavoring
¼ teaspoon cream of tartar	2 (3½-ounce) cans flaked
1 tablespoon light corn syrup	coconut
6 tablespoons water	

Combine egg whites, sugar, cream of tartar, corn syrup, and water in top of double boiler. Cook over boiling water, beating constantly with electric mixer at high speed until mixture stands in stiff peaks when beater is raised.

Stir in vanilla and coconut flavoring. Use to fill and frost three-layer cake. Cover top and sides with coconut.

❦ Coconut-Pecan Frosting

3 egg yolks	1½ cups flaked coconut
1 cup evaporated milk	1 cup chopped pecans
1 cup sugar	1 teaspoon vanilla extract
1 tablespoon butter or	
margarine	

Beat eggs and add milk, sugar, and butter or margarine. Cook over medium heat about 12 minutes, stirring constantly, until mixture thickens. Remove from heat and add coconut, pecans, and vanilla. Beat until cool and of spreading consistency. Yield: enough to cover tops of three 8- or 9-inch layers.

❦ Broiled Coconut Frosting

¼ cup butter or margarine	3 tablespoons half-and-half
½ cup brown sugar	1 cup flaked coconut

Soften the butter or margarine and blend in remaining ingredients. Spread over the top of warm or cooled cake. Place 3 inches from broiler unit. Broil until mixture bubbles and turns golden brown, about 3 to 5 minutes. Yield: enough for a 9-inch cake square.

❧ Coconut-Marshmallow Frosting

1 cup sugar	2 egg whites, stiffly beaten
½ cup boiling water	10 marshmallows, quartered
¼ teaspoon vinegar	1 cup flaked coconut

Place sugar, water, and vinegar in a saucepan and cook over low heat until sugar is dissolved. Cover, and cook for 2 minutes. Remove cover and cook until the soft ball stage is reached (238° to 240°). Pour in a thin stream over stiffly beaten egg whites, beating constantly. Add marshmallows, and continue stirring until cool and thick enough to spread. Spread on cake and sprinkle with the coconut. Yield: enough for two 8-inch layers.

❧ Fresh Coconut Frosting

3 cups granulated sugar	½ teaspoon cream of tartar
1 cup water	1 teaspoon lemon extract
2 teaspoons vinegar	1 teaspoon vanilla extract
3 egg whites, beaten	1½ cups freshly grated coconut

Stir together the sugar, water, and vinegar. Cook until it spins a fine hairlike thread. Beat egg whites with cream of tartar. Gradually add sugar mixture, beating constantly. Add lemon and vanilla extracts and mix well. Stir in coconut and spread on cooled cake layers. Yield: enough for three layers.

❧ Cola Frosting

½ cup margarine	1 box powdered sugar
3 tablespoons cocoa	1 cup chopped pecans
6 tablespoons cola drink	

Put margarine, cocoa, and cola in saucepan and bring to a boil. When margarine has melted, remove from heat and add sugar and pecans. Spread on cake. (If frosting is too stiff, add a few drops of hot water.) Yield: enough for two layers.

❧ Cream Filling

¼ cup sugar
1 tablespoon cornstarch
1 cup rich milk or cream

4 egg yolks, beaten
1½ teaspoons vanilla extract

Combine sugar, cornstarch, and milk in top of double boiler. Heat thoroughly. Pour a little of the mixture over four beaten egg yolks. Blend into hot mixture. Cook over boiling water, stirring until thick (about 2 minutes). Remove from heat and add vanilla. Chill until it sets. Spread between three layers of cake. Frost cake with favorite white, caramel, or chocolate frosting.

❧ Cooked Cream Frosting

1 cup sweet cream or
    evaporated milk
1 cup sugar
3 egg yolks, beaten
1 tablespoon butter or
    margarine

1 cup chopped nuts
1 (3½-ounce) can flaked
    coconut

Cook sweet cream, sugar, and beaten egg yolks until thick. Add butter and stir until it melts. Stir in chopped nuts and coconut. Cake can be frozen after it has the filling on it.

❧ Creamy Frosting

¼ cup butter
1 box powdered sugar
3 teaspoons strong coffee
1 egg yolk

1 teaspoon vanilla extract
1 teaspoon lemon extract
5 tablespoons cream
1 cup flaked coconut

Melt butter, add sugar and coffee, and mix well. Add egg yolk and beat. Add extracts and cream and beat at high speed until creamy, then add coconut. Yield: enough for three layers.

❦ Cream Cheese Frosting

2 (3-ounce) packages cream
  cheese
1 egg yolk
3 cups powdered sugar

⅓ teaspoon salt
1 teaspoon vanilla extract

Work the cream cheese with a fork until soft and creamy; add the egg yolk and mix well. Slowly add the sugar, mixing thoroughly after each addition. Stir in the salt and vanilla. Yield: enough for two 8-inch layers.

❦ Cream Cheese Frosting With Nuts

1 (8-ounce) package cream
  cheese, softened
½ stick margarine

1 box powdered sugar
1 teaspoon vanilla extract
Chopped pecans

Beat cream cheese and margarine until smooth; add sugar and mix well. Add vanilla and beat until smooth. Spread between layers and on top and sides of cake. Sprinkle top with pecans. Yield: enough for three 8-inch layers.

❦ Custard Filling No. 1

6 tablespoons all-purpose
  flour
1 cup sugar
¼ teaspoon salt
4 egg yolks, beaten

2 cups milk
½ teaspoon vanilla extract
⅔ cup chopped pecans, if
  desired

Mix together flour, sugar, and salt. Stir in eggs and milk. Cook, stirring constantly, until thickened. Add vanilla, cool. Stir in nuts. Yield: enough for three 9-inch layers.

❦ Custard Filling No. 2

1 cup sugar	2 cups milk
3 tablespoons cornstarch	4 egg yolks
¼ teaspoon salt	¾ cup chopped pecans

Mix sugar, cornstarch, and salt. Scald milk in top of double boiler. Beat egg yolks, add sugar mixture, then add this mixture to scalded milk. Cook 15 minutes. When cool, add pecans. Yield: enough filling to spread between three 8-inch layers.

❦ Date-Pecan Filling

1 cup sugar	½ cup chopped dates
½ cup light cream	½ cup chopped pecans
Pinch of salt	½ teaspoon vanilla extract

Combine sugar, cream, and salt together and bring to a boil. Add dates and pecans. Boil until thick and dates have been blended. Add vanilla. Cool. Yield: enough filling for two or three layers.

❦ Date Delight Filling

1½ cups chopped dates	½ cup water
¼ cup sugar	1 tablespoon lemon juice

Cook dates, sugar, and water together until thick. Cool and add lemon juice. Yield: enough filling for two layers.

❦ Divinity Frosting

1½ cups sugar	2 egg whites
6 tablespoons water	1 teaspoon vanilla extract
⅛ teaspoon cream of tartar	

Combine sugar, water, and cream of tartar. Cook syrup (without stirring) to 238° or until a small amount forms a soft ball when dropped in cold water. Pour one-third of the syrup in a fine stream over stiffly beaten egg whites, beating constantly. Cook remainder of syrup to 248°, or until a small amount forms a firm ball when dropped into cold water. Remove from heat and pour half of the remaining syrup in a fine stream into the mixture while beating constantly. Cook remaining syrup to 268°, or the hard ball stage. Remove from heat and pour last of syrup in a fine stream into the frosting, beating thoroughly. Add vanilla and beat mixture until thick enough to spread. Yield: enough for top and sides of two 9-inch layers.

❦ Fig Frosting

½ pound figs, finely chopped
⅓ cup sugar

⅓ cup boiling water
1 tablespoon lemon juice

Mix in order given and cook in top of double boiler until thick enough to spread. Spread while hot. Yield: enough for top and sides of two 8-inch layers.

❦ Japanese Fruitcake Filling

2 cups sugar
1 cup water or coconut milk
1¾ cups cake batter
   Juice and grated rind of 2
    lemons
1 large grated coconut or 2
    (3½-ounce) cans coconut

1 cup nuts
3 tablespoons melted butter or
   margarine
¼ cup green candied cherries
¼ cup candied pineapple

Combine sugar and water or coconut juice, and boil until slightly syrupy. Add the cake batter, lemon juice, and rind. Cook until thickened, stirring constantly. Then add coconut, nuts, melted butter or margarine, and candied fruits. Spread between three 8-inch layers.

❦ Grape Filling

½ cup grape juice
½ cup water
3 tablespoons cornstarch
¼ teaspoon salt

½ cup sugar
4 tablespoons lemon juice
1 tablespoon butter or
    margarine

Scald grape juice and water in top of double boiler. Combine dry ingredients and add to grape juice mixture. Cook over direct heat until thick. Return to double boiler and cook 15 minutes, stirring occasionally. Add lemon juice and butter or margarine and blend. Cool. Spread between layers of cake. Reserve ½ cup to decorate top of cake. Yield: enough filling for two 9-inch layers.

❦ Grape Frosting

1 egg white
¾ cup sugar

3 tablespoons grape juice
½ teaspoon light corn syrup

Mix all ingredients in top of double boiler and beat constantly until mixture holds a peak. Remove, and beat until thick enough to spread. Yield: enough to cover top and sides of two 9-inch layers.

❦ Easy Gelatin Frosting

1 tablespoon lemon-flavored
    gelatin
1⅓ cups powdered sugar

3 tablespoons boiling water
1 tablespoon melted butter
    Pinch of salt

Dissolve gelatin in boiling water. Add other ingredients and mix well. Yield: enough for two layers.

❦ Frosting for Jam Cake

2 cups sugar	1 cup chopped nuts
2 tablespoons all-purpose	1 cup cookie coconut
flour	1 cup chopped dates
1½ cups milk	1 cup raisins
1 cup butter	1 apple, grated

Mix sugar and flour; add milk and butter. Cook until mixture thickens, stirring occasionally. Remove from heat and stir in nuts, coconut, dates, raisins, and apple. Spread frosting between layers and over top of cake.

❦ Lady Baltimore Filling

Double recipe for Divinity Frosting. Divide frosting into halves. To one half add: 1 cup chopped seeded raisins, 1½ cups chopped nuts, 1 cup chopped figs, and ½ teaspoon lemon extract. Mix carefully, and spread between three layers of Lady Baltimore Cake. Spread remaining frosting over top and sides of cake. Sprinkle top with additional chopped figs, nuts, and raisins, if desired.

❦ Lady Baltimore Frosting

2 cups sugar	⅔ cup raisins
⅔ cup water	⅔ cup nuts
2 egg whites	Candied cherries
5 figs	

Boil sugar and water to soft ball stage (238°). Pour slowly over well-beaten egg whites, beating constantly. Set aside to cool. Put figs, raisins, and nuts through chopper. Add to cooled frosting. Spread between layers and on top and sides of three-layer cake. Garnish with nuts and halved candied cherries. Be lavish with frosting and decorations—the frosting is the show window for the cake.

❦ Lane Filling and Frosting

8 egg yolks
1¼ cups sugar
½ cup butter or margarine
1 cup chopped pecans
1 cup finely chopped raisins
1 cup flaked or fresh grated
    coconut

1 cup finely cut candied
    cherries
¼ teaspoon salt
⅓ cup fruit juice (grape,
    pineapple, or orange)

Beat egg yolks slightly; add sugar and butter. Place in saucepan and cook over medium heat, stirring constantly, for about 5 minutes, or until sugar is dissolved and mixture is slightly thickened. (Do not overcook or let egg yolks become scrambled in appearance. Mixture should be almost transparent.) Remove from heat and add remaining ingredients. Let cool before spreading on cake. Yield: enough to spread between three 8- or 9-inch layers.

❦ Filling for Lane Cake

1 cup nuts
1 cup flaked coconut
1 cup seedless raisins
½ cup butter or margarine

2 cups sugar
8 egg yolks
¾ cup grape juice

Grind nuts, coconut, and raisins. Put these in a saucepan with the butter or margarine, sugar, and egg yolks. Cook 15 to 20 minutes. Stir in grape juice to thin filling. Spread between three 9-inch layers, and use a white frosting for top and sides.

❦ Lemon-Cheese Frosting

¾ box powdered sugar
1 (8-ounce) package cream
    cheese

Pinch of salt
Juice and rind of 1 lemon
2 tablespoons evaporated milk

Mix all ingredients and heat until of spreading consistency. Yield: enough frosting for two 8- or 9-inch layers.

❧ Lemon Filling No. 1

1 cup sugar
3 tablespoons cornstarch
1 cup boiling water

2 eggs
Juice of 2 large lemons
2 tablespoons butter

Mix the sugar and cornstarch together well and add the boiling water gradually. Beat the eggs, mix with the first mixture slowly and add the lemon juice and butter. Cook, stirring constantly until it thickens. Yield: enough filling for two 8-inch layers.

❧ Lemon Filling No. 2

1 cup sugar
3 tablespoons cornstarch
½ teaspoon salt
1 cup boiling water
2 tablespoons grated lemon
 rind

½ cup lemon juice
2 tablespoons butter or
 margarine

Combine all ingredients. Bring to a full rolling boil, stirring occasionally. Turn down the heat and cook for 1 minute, stirring all the time. Let cool at room temperature. Beat well before spreading on cake. Yield: enough for two 8- or 9-inch layers.

❧ Lemon-Butter Cream Frosting

½ cup butter or margarine
4¼ cups (1-pound box) sifted
 powdered sugar
¼ teaspoon salt

1 egg white
1 teaspoon vanilla extract
1½ teaspoons grated lemon rind
1½ to 2 tablespoons lemon juice

Cream butter or margarine. Add sugar and salt alternately with egg white, beating well after each addition. Add vanilla, lemon rind, and enough lemon juice to make of spreading consistency. Add green coloring for a pale green tint, if desired. Yield: enough for two 8-inch layers.

❧ Lemon Topping

2 tablespoons cornstarch	1 tablespoon grated lemon
½ cup sugar	rind
¼ teaspoon salt	3 tablespoons lemon juice
2 cups water	¼ cup butter or margarine

Mix together cornstarch, sugar, and salt in saucepan. Gradually stir in water. Cook, stirring constantly, until mixture boils and is thick and clear. Remove from heat; stir in remaining ingredients. Serve warm. Yield: 2¼ cups sauce.

❧ Filling for Lemon Jelly Cake

1 cup sugar	6 egg yolks
3 tablespoons cornstarch	Juice of 2 lemons
½ cup hot water	⅔ stick butter or margarine
Grated rind of 2 lemons	

Cook sugar, cornstarch, water, and lemon rind together. Beat egg yolks and lemon juice. Add to other mixture, and cook until thick. Add butter or margarine, and cool before putting on layers of cake. Yield: enough filling for three 9-inch layers.

❧ Lemon Butter Filling

7 egg yolks	¼ cup lemon juice
2 cups sugar	Grated rind of 2 lemons
¼ cup all-purpose flour	1 cup butter

Beat egg yolks thoroughly. Mix sugar and flour and add to egg yolks. Add lemon juice, rind, and butter. Cook in top of double boiler, letting the water simmer but not boil. Stir constantly. Cook until mixture is thick enough to hold its shape in a spoon. Remove from heat. Beat until cool and a good consistency for spreading. May be used as a filling between layers of cake, for pies, tarts, or in éclairs. Yield: enough filling for three-layer cake.

❦ Chiffon Frosting

1 (3¾-ounce) package lemon pudding mix	1 pint heavy cream ¼ cup powdered sugar

Make lemon pudding mix as package directs. Cool slightly. Use as much as needed to frost top and sides of cake thinly. Let set. Now pour heavy cream into bowl. Whip with electric mixer or rotary beater until slightly thickened. Then add powdered sugar, 1 tablespoon at a time. Continue whipping until soft peaks form. Refrost entire cake with the cream. Garnish with paper-thin lemon slices or a border of grated lemon peel. Chill until time to serve.

❦ Filling for Lemon-Cheese Cake

2 lemons, juice and rind 3 egg yolks	½ cup butter or margarine ·1 cup sugar

Combine ingredients and cook in double boiler until thickened. Cool and spread on cake. Yield: enough filling for two 8-inch layers.

❦ Lord Baltimore Frosting

1½ cups sugar 1 tablespoon light corn syrup ½ cup water 2 egg whites, stiffly beaten ¼ teaspoon orange juice 2 teaspoons lemon juice	12 candied cherries, cut in quarters ½ cup macaroon crumbs ½ cup blanched almonds, chopped ¼ cup chopped pecans

Combine sugar, corn syrup, and water and cook until syrup forms a soft ball in cold water, or spins a long thread when dropped from tip of spoon (240°). Pour syrup in fine stream over egg whites, beating constantly. Add orange and lemon juice to fruit, macaroon crumbs, and nuts and combine the two mixtures. Cool and spread between layers of cake. Yield: enough frosting to cover tops of three 9-inch layers.

Lord Baltimore Filling

Double the recipe for Divinity Frosting and divide frosting into halves. To one half add: ½ cup dry macaroon crumbs or dry crumbled sugar cookie crumbs, ¼ cup chopped pecans, ¼ teaspoon orange extract, ¼ cup chopped blanched almonds, 12 candied cherries (cut into quarters), and 2 teaspoons lemon juice. Mix carefully and spread between three layers of Lord Baltimore Cake. Spread remaining frosting over top and sides of cake.

Marshmallow Frosting

2 egg whites
1½ cups sugar
¼ teaspoon cream of tartar
1 tablespoon light corn syrup
⅓ cup water
¼ pound marshmallows, quartered (about 16)

Combine first five ingredients in top of double boiler. Place over boiling water and cook while beating with electric mixer or rotary beater, scraping bottom and sides of pan frequently. When mixture stands in peaks, remove from heat and add marshmallows. Continue beating until frosting is thick enough to spread. Yield: enough for two 8- or 9-inch layers.

Fluffy Marshmallow Frosting

1 cup sugar
⅓ cup water
⅓ teaspoon cream of tartar
⅓ cup egg whites (about 2 eggs)
8 large marshmallows, chopped
1½ teaspoons vanilla extract

Mix sugar, water, and cream of tartar in a saucepan. Boil rapidly without stirring until mixture spins a thread when spoon is inserted and lifted above pan.

While syrup is cooking, beat egg whites until stiff; put marshmallows into hot syrup and stir until dissolved.

Pour marshmallow mixture into egg whites, beating constantly. Add vanilla and beat until stiff. Coconut may be sprinkled on frosting as a finishing touch. Yield: enough for two 8- or 9-inch layers.

❦ Molasses-Mocha Frosting

3 tablespoons molasses
3 tablespoons evaporated milk
3 teaspoons boiled coffee
4 tablespoons soft butter or
   margarine

1 teaspoon vanilla extract
About 2 cups powdered sugar
Chopped nuts

Combine all ingredients except powdered sugar and nuts. Sift sugar into liquid and beat well. Add enough sugar to make frosting the consistency to spread. Sprinkle with chopped nuts. Yield: enough to frost three 8-inch layers.

❦ Moon Glow Frosting

Grated rind of 1 lemon
4 tablespoons lemon juice
2 egg yolks, unbeaten

4½ cups powdered sugar
2 tablespoons melted butter or
   margarine

Add lemon rind and juice to the egg yolks. Stir in sugar until smooth and stiff enough to spread. Add melted butter or margarine last. Yield: enough for tops and sides of two 8-inch layers.

❦ Maclamation Cake Filling

4 egg yolks
½ cup butter
1 cup sugar

1½ cups raisins
1 cup pecans
1 cup coconut

Put eggs, butter, and sugar in saucepan, boil together until thick.

Mix raisins, pecans, and coconut and put through a food chopper. Add this mixture to the thickened egg mixture. Stir well. Cool about 5 minutes and spread on cake. Yield: enough for a two-layer cake.

❦ Never Fail Frosting

1 cup sugar	2 unbeaten egg whites
¼ teaspoon salt	3 tablespoons water
½ teaspoon cream of tartar	1 teaspoon vanilla extract

Combine all ingredients except vanilla in top of double boiler. Use mixer to stir. Beat briskly for 3 minutes or until frosting is fluffy and holds its shape. Remove and add vanilla. Yield: enough for two 9-inch layers.

❦ Orange-Coconut Frosting

3 tablespoons butter or margarine	¼ cup orange juice
2 cups powdered sugar	¾ cup flaked coconut

Cream butter until very soft. Add sugar gradually, thinning with orange juice to spreading consistency. Beat until smooth. Beat coconut into frosting. Yield: enough for two 8-inch layers.

❦ Orange Filling No. 1

1 cup sugar	2 tablespoons butter
4 tablespoons cornstarch	2 tablespoons grated orange rind
½ teaspoon salt	1½ teaspoons lemon juice
1 cup orange juice	

Mix together sugar, cornstarch, and salt. Add orange juice, butter, orange rind, and lemon juice. Bring to a boil, and boil for 5 minutes, stirring constantly. Chill before using. Yield: enough filling for two 8-inch layers.

❦ Orange Filling No. 2

1¼ cups sugar
½ cup water
2 egg whites, beaten stiff

Juice and grated rind
   of 1 orange

Boil sugar and water to form a soft ball in cup of cold water (250°). Pour in thin stream on stiffly beaten egg whites, beating all the time. Add orange juice and grated rind. Beat until cold and stiff enough to spread.

❦ Orange Frosting

3 tablespoons sugar
1 tablespoon cornstarch
½ cup evaporated milk

3 egg yolks
½ cup orange juice
1 teaspoon grated orange rind

Mix together the sugar and cornstarch in the top of a double boiler. Add the milk, and mix until smooth. Cook over hot water until slightly thickened. Beat egg yolks. Add orange juice and rind to the yolks. Stir into milk mixture. Continue cooking, stirring constantly, until thick. Cool before spreading. Yield: enough for two 8-inch layers.

❦ Orange Cloud Frosting

1 cup sugar
¼ cup orange juice
1 tablespoon grated orange
   rind

¼ cup all-purpose flour
2 eggs
¼ teaspoon salt
2 cups whipped cream

Combine sugar, juice, rind, flour, eggs, and salt in top of double boiler. Cook until thick. Cool and fold into whipped cream. Spread between three layers and over top and sides of cake.

❦ Firm Ornamental Frosting

2 (1-pound) packages
  powdered sugar
1 teaspoon cream of tartar

6 egg whites
1 teaspoon vanilla or almond
  extract

Sift the sugar and cream of tartar. Add the egg whites and mix. Add vanilla or almond. Beat until so stiff that a knife drawn through the mixture leaves a clean-cut path. This frosting is very hard. It is best used for decorating tiered wedding cakes. Yield: about 1½ cups.

❦ Ornamental Frosting

1 cup shortening
2 pounds sifted powdered
  sugar
1 unbeaten egg white

½ teaspoon salt
1 teaspoon vanilla extract
⅓ to ½ cup lukewarm cream

Cream the shortening and a part of the sugar gradually. Add the egg white, salt, and vanilla. Then alternately add the cream and the remaining sugar. Beat until fluffy and creamy. This makes a large amount of icing which will keep in a tight container in the refrigerator. May be used for cake decorating. Yield: about 3 cups.

❦ Decorating Butter Cream

2 cups vegetable shortening
1 cup powdered sugar

½ cup egg whites
1 cup granulated sugar

Cream shortening and powdered sugar in electric mixer until light and fluffy; remove to largest bowl of mixer. Heat egg whites and granulated sugar in double boiler to 150° (be sure to use candy thermometer; exact temperature is important). Then whip for several minutes on medium-high speed to make a thick meringue. Add half of meringue to first mixture and beat for about 10 minutes. Add rest of meringue and beat at medium-high speed until icing holds its shape. Add flavoring and coloring as desired. May be used for frosting cakes and for making decorations. Keep stored in covered container in refrigerator until ready for use. Yield: about 3 cups.

❦ Peanut Butter Frosting

2 tablespoons butter or margarine	3½ cups powdered sugar
¼ cup peanut butter	About 6 tablespoons milk

Blend butter and peanut butter together. Add powdered sugar and enough milk to make frosting soft enough to spread. Decorate top of cake with pitted dates. Yield: enough to cover top and sides of two 8-inch layers.

❦ Peanut Butter Broiled Frosting

⅔ cup brown sugar	4 tablespoons cream
4 tablespoons soft butter or margarine	4 tablespoons peanut butter
	1 cup chopped peanuts

Mix all ingredients together and spread on cold cake. Place about 3 inches under the broiler until mixture browns. Yield: enough for top of a 13- x 9-inch cake.

❦ Pecan Broiled Frosting

6 tablespoons soft butter or margarine	4 tablespoons cream
¾ cup brown sugar	½ cup pecans, chopped

Mix all ingredients together and spread on top of warm cake. Place about 3 inches under the broiler until mixture browns. Yield: enough for top of 13- x 9-inch cake.

🍃 Pineapple Filling No. 1

4 egg yolks
½ cup sugar
⅓ cup cornstarch

½ cup hot water
Juice of 1 lemon
1 small can crushed pineapple

Blend all ingredients well and cook over low heat in top of double boiler until thickened. Cool, then spread between three 8- or 9-inch layers. Frost with a cooked white frosting.

🍃 Pineapple Filling No. 2

1 (8¼-ounce) can crushed
   pineapple
2 eggs
1 cup sugar
3 tablespoons all-purpose
   flour

1 tablespoon butter
1 tablespoon lemon juice
1 cup coconut

Mix the first four ingredients in top of double boiler. Cook the mixture until thickened. Take from heat and add butter, lemon juice, and coconut. Mix well and set aside to cool. Spread between three layers.

🍃 Petits Fours Frosting

6 cups sifted powdered sugar
5 tablespoons water

5 tablespoons corn syrup
1 teaspoon vanilla extract

Mix powdered sugar, water, corn syrup, and vanilla and heat just to lukewarm in top of double boiler. Remove from heat, leaving over lukewarm water to keep frosting soft while covering Petits Fours. Use food coloring to tint part of frosting delicate pastel colors. Do not overheat frosting or it will become dull. Yield: about 4 cups.

Note: If mixture begins to thicken while frosting Petits Fours, reheat. Leftover frosting can be reheated and reused.

❧ Pineapple Frosting No. 1

2 cups sugar
1 stick margarine
1 cup evaporated milk
1 teaspoon vanilla extract

1 cup flaked coconut
1 (13½-ounce) can crushed
   pineapple, drained
1 cup chopped nuts

Combine sugar, margarine, and evaporated milk in a saucepan. Cook over low heat or in top of double boiler until thick, stirring often. When mixture thickens, add vanilla, coconut, pineapple (drained), and chopped nuts. Cook 10 to 15 minutes longer. Cool. Yield: enough for tops and sides of two 8-inch layers.

❧ Pineapple Frosting No. 2

¼ cup sugar
1 tablespoon cornstarch
   Dash of salt
⅔ cup pineapple juice
2 slightly beaten egg yolks

1 tablespoon butter or
   margarine
1 cup drained crushed
   pineapple

Combine sugar, cornstarch, and salt in a saucepan. Add the pineapple juice to the slightly beaten egg yolks and blend. Then add gradually to the sugar mixture, mixing thoroughly. Place over medium heat and bring to a boil, stirring constantly. Remove from heat. Add butter or margarine and pineapple. Mix well. Cool before spreading on cake. Yield: enough for tops and sides of two 8-inch layers.

❧ Prune Whip Cake Filling

2 tablespoons unflavored gelatin
½ cup liquid from cooked
   prunes
¼ cup sugar

2 cups cooked, pitted, mashed
   prunes
1 cup cream, whipped

Cut two 8-inch layer cakes into four thin layers. Soften gelatin in prune liquid and dissolve over hot water. Stir gelatin and sugar into cooked prunes. Cool until slightly thickened, then combine with whipped cream. Yield: enough filling for three-layer cake.

❦ Peppermint Frosting

5 tablespoons cold water	1 teaspoon vanilla extract
1 tablespoon white corn syrup	Red coloring
1½ cups sugar	½ cup crushed peppermint
¼ teaspoon cream of tartar	candy
2 egg whites	

Combine all ingredients except vanilla, red coloring, and candy, and mix well. Set over rapidly boiling water and beat constantly until mixture will hold a soft peak. Remove from heat and set over cold water. Add vanilla, and beat until mixture will hold a sharp peak. This frosting does not get hard or grainy. Add the cake coloring and the peppermint candy just before spreading. Yield: enough for two 8-inch layers.

❦ Pudding Mix Frosting

1 (3¾-ounce) package vanilla-flavored pudding mix	Milk
	1 cup cream for whipping

Prepare pudding mix with milk, following label directions. Cover; cool completely. Beat cream until stiff in small bowl; fold into cooled pudding mixture. Put cake layers together on serving plate with pudding mixture between and on top. Chill several hours, or overnight. Yield: two cups.

❦ Raisin Cream Filling

1 cup sugar	1 cup chopped raisins
1 cup thin cream	3 eggs, well beaten
¼ teaspoon salt	1 tablespoon butter
2 tablespoons all-purpose flour	

Mix ingredients and cook until thick in top of double boiler. Stir often to prevent sticking. Cool, and spread between two 9-inch layers and on top of cake.

❧ Raisin Frosting

1½ cups seedless raisins, chopped
¾ cup water
¼ cup molasses
2 tablespoons cornstarch

½ teaspoon ground cinnamon
¼ teaspoon ground cloves
1 tablespoon butter or
  margarine
½ teaspoon grated lemon rind

Grind the raisins in a food chopper twice, using the coarsest blade. Add water, molasses, cornstarch, and spices. Mix well. Cook until the mixture is thick and clear, stirring constantly. Stir in butter or margarine and lemon rind. Yield: enough filling for two 9-inch layers.

❧ Rum Filling

⅔ cup butter
½ cup rum

2½ cups sifted powdered sugar

Mix all ingredients thoroughly and set in refrigerator to thicken. Put between layers and put cake in refrigerator to set filling before frosting. Frost with your favorite frosting, using rum for flavoring. Yield: enough filling for two 8-inch layers.

❧ Seafoam Frosting No. 1

2 egg whites
1½ cups brown sugar, firmly
  packed

⅓ cup water
⅛ teaspoon salt
1 teaspoon vanilla extract

Combine egg whites, brown sugar, water, and salt in top of double boiler. Place over boiling water. Beat constantly with rotary beater or electric mixer until frosting will hold a peak, about 7 minutes. Remove from hot water and add vanilla. Continue to beat until stiff enough to spread. Yield: enough to fill and frost two 8-inch layers.

❧ Seafoam Frosting No. 2

⅓ cup sugar
⅓ cup brown sugar, firmly
    packed
⅓ cup water

1 tablespoon corn syrup
1 egg white
¼ teaspoon cream of tartar

Combine in saucepan sugar, brown sugar, water, and corn syrup. Cook until a little syrup dropped in cold water forms a soft ball (236°). Meanwhile, beat egg white with cream of tartar until stiff peaks form. Add syrup to egg white in slow, steady stream, beating constantly, until thick enough to spread. Yield: enough to cover top of one 9-inch layer.

❧ Seven-Minute Frosting

3 tablespoons water
1 egg white
1 tablespoon corn syrup or
⅛ teaspoon cream of tartar

1 cup sugar
⅛ teaspoon salt
1 teaspoon vanilla extract

Heat water to boiling in lower part of double boiler. Water in lower part should surround upper part. Place water, egg white, syrup or cream of tartar, sugar, and salt in upper part of double boiler. Beat the mixture with a rotary egg beater or electric beater, rapidly at first, then steadily and continuously for about 7 minutes. Keep water boiling in lower part of double boiler during the beating. Remove from heat, pour out hot water and fill with cold water, and replace upper part of double boiler. Allow it to stand 5 minutes. Add flavoring and stir.

Variations: *Brown Sugar Frosting:* Substitute 1 cup brown sugar for white sugar, use 2 tablespoons water in place of 3 tablespoons. Omit corn syrup or cream of tartar. *Fruit and Nut Frosting:* Add ½ cup nuts, figs, dates, or raisins, or a combination of these. *Coconut Frosting:* Coconut may be mixed with frosting or sprinkled on top.

❦ Strawberry Frosting

1 box powdered sugar
¼ stick butter

½ cup fresh strawberries or
   drained frozen
   strawberries, chopped

Beat ingredients thoroughly. Spread between layers and on top of three 8-inch layers.

❦ Boiled Taffy Frosting

2 cups sugar
½ cup water
¼ cup molasses
   Dash of salt

2 egg whites, beaten
1 teaspoon vanilla extract

Thoroughly mix the sugar, water, molasses, and salt. Cook without stirring to the firm ball stage (245°). Gradually add the hot syrup to the beaten egg whites, beating all the time. Continue beating until mixture stands in high peaks. Beat in vanilla. If frosting hardens before spreading, beat in a few drops of hot water. Yield: enough for tops and sides of two 9-inch layers.

❦ Powdered Sugar Frosting

Whites of 3½ eggs
4 cups powdered sugar
3 cups soft butter
1 teaspoon vanilla extract

1 teaspoon lemon extract
Dash of salt
½ cup chopped nuts (optional)

For the icing, beat egg whites; add sugar gradually, then add butter, vanilla extract, and lemon extract. Add salt. Mix thoroughly. If desired, sprinkle top of iced cake with chopped nuts. Yield: enough for three 9-inch layers.

❧ Vanilla Cream Frosting

2 envelopes unflavored gelatin
½ cup cold water
2 cups milk, scalded
¾ cup sugar
4 egg yolks, beaten

1½ teaspoons vanilla extract
1 cup heavy cream, whipped
⅓ cup grated coconut
Tinted coconut for garnish

Soften gelatin in cold water. Add gelatin to hot milk and mix well. Stir in sugar. Heat, but do not boil; pour over beaten egg yolks, stirring constantly. Blend in vanilla and set aside to cool. Chill until mixture begins to thicken. Fold in whipped cream and grated coconut and pour over cake. Refrigerate until set and ready to serve. To serve, remove sides of pan. Place on a large serving plate, and sprinkle with tinted coconut. Yield: enough for three 8-inch layers.

❧ White Frosting

6 tablespoons all-purpose
  flour
1 cup water
1 cup butter

1 cup granulated sugar
1 teaspoon vanilla extract

Cook the flour and water until slightly clear. Cool for at least 2 hours. Cream the butter, sugar, and vanilla, and add to cool flour mixture. Beat with electric beater until light and fluffy. Yield: enough for two 8-inch layers.

Index

Index